中央财经大学"双一流"建设国际税收项目　中央财经大学标志性科研成果培育项目
百年变局中的国际税收改革

马海涛　总主编

REFORM OF
INTERNATIONAL
TAX
GOVERNANCE
IN THE DIGITAL
ECONOMY

数字经济
国际税收治理
变　革

1

理论、战略与政策篇
THEORY, STRATEGY AND POLICY

曹明星　著

社会科学文献出版社
SOCIAL SCIENCES ACADEMIC PRESS (CHINA)

丛书序

当今世界正经历百年未有之大变局，数字化转型成为经济发展的新引擎。数字经济背景下，市场国征税权成为国际税收秩序世纪变革的重大战略变量。市场国征税权的兴起，使得当前的国际税收改革大大超越了原来的全球反避税范畴，谋求国际税收公平以改变国际经济失衡的单边、双边和多边规则，正在欧美主导的博弈中不断出台。而身为发展中国家且已是全球数字经济大国的中国，目前在税基安全、公平和发展的多重复杂目标下面临诸多抉择困惑。面对数字经济下国际税收管辖权分配的变化与创新，我们需要重新认知环境、明确立场，因为市场国征税权的竞争，关乎国家税收利益、世界产业格局，将极大地影响未来全球政治经济格局的塑造。

"数字经济国际税收治理变革"系列研究尝试对上述

问题做出初步解答。研究形成了三部在逻辑上构成整体而又各自自成体系的成果，分别是"理论、战略与政策篇""挑战、应对与机制篇""案例、专题与评注篇"。

第一部首先从政府贡献视角大胆对国家和国际税收基础理论进行创新，其次力图构造与升级经合组织的税基侵蚀与利润转移（BEPS）反避税战略，打造适应"一带一路"倡议的税基共建与利润共享（New-BEPS）国际税收合作战略，最后尝试厘清税收与经济利益的中国关切，并提出应对数字经济国际税收治理变革的中国方案。

第二部在全面认识数字经济本质和当前国际税收秩序的基础上，首先探寻当前国际税制落后于数字经济的矛盾焦点，其次剖析参与其中的各相关方采取的对策和专家学者给出的建议，最后给出税基共建与利润共享（New-BEPS）战略具体落地的安排。

第三部从纷繁芜杂的社会现实中搜寻关于数字经济国际税收改革的相关新闻和案例资料，从不同侧面认识当前的矛盾以及各方采取的对策，了解相关专家学者的建议，以对当前的数字经济国际税收改革全景有更清晰的认知。

"数字经济国际税收治理变革"系列研究，是本人和曹明星老师在中国财政发展协同创新中心规划的国际税收跨学科团队重点研究项目，是中央财经大学标志性研究成果之一，研究过程中得到李涛教授基于互联网与数字经济领域、白彦锋教授基于数字经济财税领域、林光彬教授基于政治经济学领域、白云真教授基于中国传统文化领域提供的专业咨询，他们的指导和建议对于研究视野的拓宽、研究内容的深化和研究成果的形成均有重大帮助，在此特致谢意！

虽然如此，我们还必须认识到，关于数字经济国际税收治理变革问题的研究，是当前哲学社会科学研究的前沿点和交叉点，显然也是困难点，无论是对于数字经济本质和特点的科学挖掘，对于国际税收基础理论创新的精心研究和继续深化，对于国际税收治理战略的建构和升级，还是对于国际税收治理变革中国政策应对策略的制定，都有极大的益处；加之经合组织改革方案框架已经出台，为了引起更多的讨论并形成更好的政策建议，在时间仓促、所虑甚多而着笔有限的情况下，本系列研究尝试抛出对这一重大全球治理问题的初步理解，问题肯定很多，错漏必然不少，欢迎业界专家和社会各界提出批评修改建议，以待我们后续改进完善。

马海涛

2022 年 3 月 12 日

前　言

　　国际税收治理无疑是当今世界发展变革的重要枢纽之一。在中国特色发展进入新时代之际，世界同样面临着百年变局中的发展不平衡问题和数字经济新阶段的发展不充分问题；在国际税收领域，无论是作为金融危机之后世界格局变化标志之一的国际反避税共识的迅速达成，还是目前全球层面数字经济国际税收治理机制的博弈建构，均事关利益之争和格局之争，影响未来长期发展，极大地凸显了国际税收治理作为世界政治、经济和社会格局转换调整核心点和突破点的历史意义。由此，百年变局中对国际税收治理变革的理论解释与机制建构，能否解决好国际税收发展的不平衡和不充分问题，直接关系现代化进程中中国与世界关系的历史定位，将具有很好的标本性、示范性价值和意义。

数字经济国际税收治理变革研究的成功关键在于对世界经济背景的解析与数字税改挑战的梳理。一是深刻把握百年变局中的世界经济格局背景，对世界经济经历的大发展、大调整和大变局的历史逻辑进行科学阐释，对中华民族复兴和社会主义重振的历史时点进行准确定位；同时，深刻挖掘数字经济时空聚合的规模性、跨界性特质，界定其在全球化新时代中的战略变量本质，并评估其对世界经济发展加速和格局调整加剧可能产生的历史效应。二是全面梳理数字税改中的国际税收治理挑战，直面数字经济下国际税收管辖权分配规则的多重冲击，解析从理论基础、基本原则到治理机制等各个层面所面临的困境，继而深入观察国际税收治理从双边到多边机制演进的本质特征，前瞻国际税收全球性治理机制探索的未来趋势。

数字经济国际税收治理变革研究的第一主题是理论创新。一是对数字经济背景下的国际税收治理大胆进行理论发掘，在国家层面对市场经济中的国家税收理论进行再思考，从政府贡献视角补全可比交易全景，重新论证国家/政府税收的正当性及其边界；二是在国际层面考虑跨境交易中的国际税收管辖权再分配，在国际贸易和国际投资等环节创新利润生成和分配机制，平衡生产国和市场国、居民国和来源国的税收利益和权利。

数字经济国际税收治理变革研究的第二主题是战略

选择。首先是经合组织提出的应对跨国公司税基侵蚀与利润转移（BEPS）的反避税战略，指明其受税收狭义化影响而导致的国家财政失败，以及由此带来的改革进步性与局限性；其次是中国基于"一带一路"倡议的共商共建共享原则，推动建立税基共建与利润共享（New-BEPS）国际税收合作发展战略，阐明其避免税收脱嵌化、营造有利于全面经济发展的改革理念的先进性。

数字经济国际税收治理变革研究的第三主题是政策设计。一是深入剖析数字经济国际税收改革方案的全球博弈。首先针对典型国家提出的数字服务税的单边主义措施，阐明历史正当性、反思规则可行性和治理争议性；同时集中精力探析经合组织基于多边合作框架提出的双支柱改革方案，分析其在谋求市场国公平税收权益的同时限制了新兴行业/落后地区的财政自主权和发展公平权，指明其改革的进步性与保守性，并进行利益再平衡和规则再建构。二是科学建构数字经济国际税收改革的中国应对之策。首先阐明中国作为社会主义数字经济市场大国，对数字经济国际税收改革在税基安全、公平和发展三个方面的全面关切，强调系统建构、内外联动，实现税收与经济的"双循环"发展格局；其次着重勾画数字经济国际税收改革的中国方案，建立基于全球市场竞争与政府合作的技术机制和规则体系，打破霸权主义全球化，打造有利于多边主义区域一体化和"一带一路"建设的新格局。

长期以来，国际税收理论研究和政策制定还主要是在西方理念和话语框架下展开的，理论和实践均表现出很多基于资本主义和市场主义的物化性及微观竞争特点；数字经济下，从短缺经济到过剩经济，权利配置主导方发生变化，很多误区要重新认知。本书研究基于中国思维，兼采政治经济学分析方法，探索从本质层面解析数字经济背景下全球产业链和价值链失衡，以及市场国征税权兴起的根本原因，有利于从经济和法律相结合的分析路径，全面解析当前国际税改方案中市场国征税权规则设置的利弊，从而形成在数字经济下国际税收秩序变革新阶段中国应对策略的要点与逻辑体系。

本书是"数字经济国际税收治理变革"系列研究的第一部，对新时代国际税收治理变革提出了独到的见解。无论是对新阶段的认知、对新理念的建构还是对新格局的前瞻，均试图透过具体的财经和政法现象，发掘其背后更为深刻的理论本质和实践逻辑。一是着力解决国际税收全球治理新阶段的原理创新与继承问题，弥合现有改革方案说理不足和不清的缺陷，提供有价值的理论解决方案；二是尝试提出国际税收全球治理的战略基础与战略升级问题，解决税基侵蚀与利润转移（BEPS）战略与"一带一路"税基共建与利润共享战略的沟通和衔接问题，提供目标清晰的战略发展方向。

一方面，本书对国际税收治理新阶段和新理念提出了较为深刻科学的理论解释。基于人们在不同层次类共同体中的公私利益博弈，从更大范围、更长链条和更深程度上，解释清楚全球化失衡和国家利益的觉醒；并在更宽广视角重构跨境交易多维框架的基础上，提出了更为可信的国家税收正当性和数量边界理论，支持了更为合理的"供需双方创造利润"学说，为数字经济条件下的市场国征税权提供理论依据，从而为生产国、市场国及跨国公司多方平衡发展的新秩序奠定基础。

另一方面，本书为国际税收治理新理念和新格局设计了较为完整系统的应对方案。在论证了经合组织提出的税基侵蚀与利润转移（BEPS）行动计划主要是基于反避税、保护发达国家税基的根本理念之后，指出其框架下的数字经济国际税收改革仅仅是一种有限的形式公平的政策机制；与之对应，本书阐明了中国的"一带一路"倡议将催生税基共建与利润共享（New-BEPS）战略机制，努力实现包括数字经济在内的全球经济循环中的税基安全、公平和发展的系统平衡，以及有利于发展中国家经济社会发展的更具全面性和公平性的秩序的建构。

目　录

001　第一章　数字经济国际税收治理变革的机制挑战
001　　第一节　传统国际税收治理的格局变动与数字经济的挑战
002　　　一　传统国际税收治理的格局变动
007　　　二　数字经济对国际税收治理的机制挑战
012　　第二节　数字经济国际税收变革中的全球治理机制探索
012　　　一　数字经济背景下国际税收规则变革的初步依据
020　　　二　数字经济背景下国际税收机制变革的基本趋势

026　第二章　数字经济国际税收治理变革的理论创新
026　　第一节　政府贡献与市场经济中的国家税收依据再思考
027　　　一　政府与价值创造的关系
030　　　二　价值创造与利益分配错位
033　　　三　现有利益分配规则的困境
037　　　四　以政府贡献重构国际税收新秩序

038	第二节 供需利润与跨境交易中的国际税收管辖权再分配
038	一 国际税收管辖权分配的理论依据
045	二 跨境交易的剩余利润分配新征税权规则
050	三 全球防止税基侵蚀方案的规则再建构
055	结语

056	**第三章 数字经济国际税收治理变革的战略选择**
056	第一节 应对税基侵蚀与利润转移（BEPS）反避税战略
057	一 BEPS 反避税战略的背景与框架
059	二 BEPS 反避税战略的本质与问题
064	第二节 推动税基共建与利润共享（New-BEPS）合作发展战略
064	一 "一带一路"新发展格局与数字经济发展新需求
071	二 数字经济时代"一带一路"国际税收治理的中国思路

076	**第四章 数字经济国际税收治理变革的政策设计**
076	第一节 数字经济国际税收治理变革的国际博弈
077	一 数字服务税的单边主义措施
087	二 双支柱方案的多边合作框架
099	第二节 数字经济国际税收治理变革的中国应对
100	一 数字经济国际税收治理变革的战略背景

101 二 数字经济国际税收治理变革的政策要点
106 三 数字经济国际税收治理变革的政策机制设计

110 参考文献

115 附录

第一章
数字经济国际税收治理变革的机制挑战

新时代国际税收治理要立足于世界经济背景的解析与数字税改的挑战。首先要把握世界经济格局背景，深刻挖掘数字经济时空聚合的规模性、跨界性特质，界定其在全球化新时代中的战略变量本质，以及其对世界经济发展加速和格局调整加剧可能产生的历史效应。其次是全面梳理数字税改中的国际税收治理挑战，直面数字经济下国际税收管辖分配规则多重挑战，分析从理论基础、基本原则到治理机制等各个层面所面临的困境，继而深入观察国际税收治理从双边到多边机制演进的本质特征，前瞻国际税收全球性治理机制的趋势。

第一节 传统国际税收治理的格局变动 与数字经济的挑战

在国际税收治理基础确立和框架定型之后，传统国际税收的发展和当前世界经济失衡一样，正经历着困境；数字经济的异军突起和蓬勃发展,对经济和税收发展的不平衡、不充分提出新的变革需求。

一 传统国际税收治理的格局变动

(一)国际税收治理的秩序困境

自 2008 年国际金融危机爆发到 2020 年新冠肺炎疫情全球蔓延,世界经济重心由大西洋两岸开始向太平洋两岸转移,逆全球化现象频发,全球化进程和世界经济、政治格局正在经历着大变革,不同政治体系及各国治理水平的矛盾凸显。随着数字经济时代的到来,传统的生产组织形式发生了剧变,新的价值创造要素改变了各国跨境贸易的方式,促使世界经济完成新旧动能的转换,加剧了各国经济发展的失衡及传统国际税收规则失效的困境。

自 2012 年研究开始到 2015 年正式实施,G20 领导下的以防止"税基侵蚀与利润转移"(Base Erosion and Profit Shifting,BEPS)为核心的国际税收规则秩序在一定程度上维持了各个国家税基的稳定。随着多边合作的深入开展及BEPS 行动计划在各国的相继落地,国际税收治理秩序进入"后 BEPS 时代"。回顾国际税收治理秩序的变革之路,其规则演变呈现以下几个基本特征。一是对政府角色的认识相对固化。当下国际税收规则遵循的用以划分税权的"经济关联原则"（Nexus）及确定税基的"独立交易原则"（Arm's Length Principle）本质上反映的是一种单一的税收权基础和单一的政府与市场关系，即税收是政府对私人部门财富创造的一种单向汲取。在竞争机制的市场经济中，政府只是扮演着消极的"守夜人"角色，以私人部门在社会再生产过程中的独立交易结果作为征税基础。二是对治理路径的探究存在断层。对国际税收治理秩序的探究本应沿着"为何征、由谁征、征多少"的思路对税权基础、税权划分和税基界定进行递进分析和讨论，但当前应对数字经济税改的方案缺少对税权基础这一根本问题的深入思考，而是直接尝试从税权分配这一层面解决数字经济税收挑战带来的问题，其后果是再周全的方案设计也只能达到扬汤止沸的效果。三是对规则重构的观察视角较为片面。从BEPS行动计划到应对数字经济税收挑战的双支柱方案，观察视角仍是从市场出发，仅围绕"私人部门"在生产交换及价值创造过程中的核心地位进行税权划分、税基确定，忽略了政府所扮演的"福利国家""有为政府"等角色在税权归属中的价值创造功能，直接导致在对国际税收规则进行重构时对关键问题和核心矛盾解读与认知的片面性和局限性。[1] 以上三个特征表明，在当

---

[1] 杜建伟，曹明星. 国际税收治理变革的几个基本问题探讨——数字经济下的税收权力、价值创造、公私交换与税基确定 [J]. 国际税收，2021（01）：14-19.

前以欧美发达国家为主导的数字经济国际税改建构中，以单一的私人部门为视角的理论基础及以"经济关联原则"和"独立交易原则"为核心的治理实践在努力维护资本输出国税收利益的同时，忽视了垄断资本的全球化态势，这种治理秩序困境面临着严峻的矛盾和挑战。

（二）国际税收治理参与力量发生变化

在传统国际税收治理秩序中，以美国为代表的西方发达国家是主导者和主要参与者，自1923年荷兰、意大利、英国和美国的四位经济学家发布《防止双重征税报告》形成国际税收规则以来，发达资本主义国家始终把控着议题探讨、人事任命等方面的国际税收规则制定权，因此传统国际税收体系难以避免得偏向维护发达国家所代表的居民国和资本输出国的税收利益。[1] 在这一进程中，发展中国家由于力量薄弱，只能被动接受国际税收规则，只有十分有限的话语权。而随着发展中国家的逐渐崛起，经济规模逐渐扩大，在国际平台上的地位不断提高，相应地要求在国际税收规则制定上享有更多的话语权。2013年启动的BEPS行动计划将更多的发展中国家和新兴经济体纳入规

---

[1] 罗秦.国际税收治理从双边到多边的演进：新格局、新挑战及新趋势[J].国际税收，2021（01）.

则制定的范围，给予其表达税收利益诉求的权利，这表明发展中国家和新兴经济体在国际税收秩序中开始占有不容忽视的比重，发达国家只有协调好与发展中国家的税收利益分配关系才能更好地提高税收现代化水平。国家力量对比的变化使得国际税收治理秩序逐渐走向"全球化"的税收治理秩序，将达到新的平衡。

（三）数字经济国际税收治理变革的新要求

随着经济全球化和数字经济的快速发展，新的生产要素参与收益分配，各国投资和贸易的形式发生了改变，各国税收治理工具及国际税收利益划分都面临着较大的问题。此外，区块链、涉税信息收集处理等技术的发展与变革，推动税收征管数字化转型。对于数字经济带来的这些新问题，应该看到以下重大趋势。

为了共同应对数字经济税收的挑战，国家之间的合作踏上了新的征程。自 2015 年土耳其 G20 峰会将国际税收合作纳入"增强抗风险能力"板块，与金融风险监控等国际合作并列后，[1] 2016 年杭州峰会联合发布《二十国集团数字经济发展与合作倡议》，至 2019 年大阪峰会主要领导人共同签署《大阪数字经济宣言》，都展现了包括发达国家

---

[1] 加强全球税收治理是大事 [N]. 中国财经报，2015-12-01（006）.

和发展中国家在内的全球主要经济体对于加强应对数字经济税收挑战的共同合作的认可和重视,这是当下世界的主流趋势和不可逆的潮流。

在应对数字经济税收挑战进程中,也应当认识到主权国家间利益的不平衡和竞争依然是常态。其根本原因在于税收属于一国之内的主权,任何凌驾于国家税收主权之上的干预行为必然不可能一帆风顺,多边协调下的国际税收治理秩序难以避免地会面临困境。这是迄今为止尚不能协调各国税收利益关系的原因,也是未来尝试应对国际税收竞争格局的长期制度性挑战。当前,美国位居全球数字经济竞争力排名之首,中国紧随其后,欧盟、日韩等发达经济体和其他新兴经济体也在数字经济的潮流下奋起直追。数字经济实力是国家实力的重要体现,数字经济税收规则的制定也是各国利益博弈的重要过程。从2019年至今,应对数字经济税收挑战的双支柱方案尚未最终成型,多国已相继出台单边税收措施,以法国、土耳其为首的多个国家开征数字服务税(Digital Service Tax,DST)以维护自身的核心税收利益,使得针对特定大型跨国企业的侵害性征税加剧了全球税负的不均衡。由此可见,在数字经济时代达成国际税收治理秩序合作共识的难度很大,税收"逆全球化"现象及税收单边主义倾向难以得到根本遏制。

在这种利益竞争格局下,必须首先站在国家利益的角度思考问题。要在公平推进数字经济税收利润分配规则谈判、弥合各国发展鸿沟等议题上加强国际交流与合作，同时，权衡和把握好适应数字经济国际税改的主流趋势以及维护好我国在数字经济时代的税收权益，以发展我国数字经济为目标，保护国家税收和经济利益。

二 数字经济对国际税收治理的机制挑战

数字经济对国际税收形成艰巨挑战的根本原因在于，数字经济加剧了全球经济中的供需失衡，但因为国际税收管辖权设置的先在缺陷，无法提供公平有效的国际税基分割机制。数字经济有价值链、价值平台和价值商店三种不同商业模式，改变了跨国公司全球价值链构建和利润生成机制，其具有的跨辖区高度流动、增规模减实体、极度依赖无形资产、数据成为核心生产要素、用户参与和数据的价值贡献更加重要等显著性特征，加剧了税基侵蚀与利润转移（BEPS）问题的产生和发展。

在经合组织的 BEPS 行动计划中，核心思想是提出并坚持"利润应在经济活动发生地和价值创造地被征税"的基本理念，但由此也导致支撑现行国际税收规则判定标准的两大基石在数字经济条件下受到根本性挑战：一是确定何处征税的"经济关联原则"，在缺乏物理存在的情形下难以确定税收管辖权；二是确定如何征税的"独立交易原则"，在无法确定用户参与和数据对价值创造贡献的情形下难以确定利润的归属。最终，人们甚至对国际税收关于征税主体、征税对象、征税方式乃至税种性质均产生重大疑问。

（一）经济关联原则难题

数字经济下传统关联因素与新经济形态之间存在错配现象。

数字经济对税收管辖权和税基分割理念与规则形成的挑战，需要我们重新理解基本概念并实现本质的联通。国际税收规则以关联因素为基础，将税收管辖权划分为两大原则，即属人原则和属地原则。在属人原则下，将本国居民的税收管辖权全部授予一国，一国有权对该国居民的全球所得进行征税；在属地原则下，一国仅对非居民来源于该国的所得进行征税。这两项原则都以"经济关联原则"来对居民身份及收入来源进行认定，例如，通过鉴别永久性住所、重要利益中心等标准识别自然人的居民身份，通过公司注册地、实际管理机构所在地等标准识别法人的居民身份。然而，在数字经济商业模式下，跨国企业可以利用信息通信技术实现跨境交易，业务经营不再必然依赖真实物理存在的经营实体，这导致以物理存在作为判定标准的传统关联原则越来越模糊,难以真实反映数字经济下价值创造与价值分配的实质。①

尤其是对常设机构的认定标准可以反映传统国际税收关联原则与数字经济形态之间产生的错配。关联原则在识别常设机构时对质和量都分别做出了规定,即企业要具有可以进行营业的分支机构等固定营业场所,辅助性和准备性的营业活动被排除在认定标准之外。但随着新经济形态的发展,很多跨国企业利用常设机构规则认定的漏洞,通过税收筹划避免在来源国形成物理存在的经营实体,特别是很多互联网公司仅通过辅助性或准备性的活动即可在来源国创造大量价值,获取巨额收益而免于重税。尽管 BEPS 行动计划对常设机构增加了新的排除豁免规则,但本质上仍是依赖于物理存在的关联原则,难以将跨国企业不依赖经营实体即可攫取来源国税收利益的情形考虑在内。因此,以物理存在作为关联因素的现行国际税收管辖规则难以支撑数字经济的发展,甚至成为市场国获取征税权的阻碍。

数字经济下跨境交易的所得定性存在不确定性。

现行以关联因素为基础的国际税收规则将跨境交易所得按照交易方式及性质的不同划分为四种类型,分别是经

---

① 励贺林. 对数字经济商业模式下收益归属国际税收规则的思考 [J]. 税务研究,2018(07).

营所得、劳务所得、财产转让所得及投资所得，不同类型的所得所适用的税率、征管方式、所属来源国等都不尽一致。而随着数字经济下商业模式的不断发展与革新，企业资产形态正在悄然改变，实体资产正在加快数字化转型。价值创造模式的变革促进了资产货币化的转变，跨境交易收益的获取手段和分享机制相应发生了改变，由此导致了各种类型所得的分类和定性愈加困难。[①] 例如，现在互联网公司通过远程数据传输的形式向他国提供互联网广告服务，这种跨境交易所得被认定为来源国的营业所得或者非居民的特许权使用费所得，这种认定在数字经济背景下是有争议的。

（二）利润归属难题

关联原则和新经济形态之间的错配产生了一项新的难题，即利润归属的判断难题。由于数字经济商业模式的改变，企业获得收益的途径和往常不同，不再遵循传统价值创造的模式。此外，数字经济下广泛使用的信息通信技术具有高度的移动性，传统的属人原则和属地原则不再适用，如何在市场国与生产国之间分配利润成为一大难题。

---

① 崔虹.拨开迷雾：数字经济下税收管辖分配规则三重挑战的应对[J]. 国际经济法学刊，2020（04）.

更困难的是,数字经济下交易对象的实质是以知识产权为核心的无形资产,而无形资产因其不具有实物形态、公允价值难以确定等特点,成为跨国公司利用转让定价实现避税的一大工具。跨国公司可以通过关联交易、成本分摊、授权许可等方式,转移无形资产所产生的收益,这种情况很难判断利润归属,利润归属难题也由此而产生了。

为解决上述问题,OECD也做出了回应。根据协定范本的规定,在确定常设机构的利润归属时,通常依据独立实体法作为基础的判定方法。在具体运用独立实体法时,通常包括如下两个步骤。首先,假定目标常设机构是独立的企业,对其进行功能分析。分析的内容包括其所承担的功能、风险,以及拥有的无形资产、有形资产和执行重要活动的人员。其次,在得到功能分析的结果后,比对类似情况下的交易,采用适当的转让定价方法对利润归属进行判定和分配。通常情况下,OECD建议采用可比非受控价格法对交易进行可比性分析,进而确认利润归属。

虽然OECD看似提出了进行利润归属判定的可供参考的解决方案,但仍存在两点明显的缺陷。第一,在功能分析时,由于数字经济的分散性、可移动性和快速演变等特点,如何在企业的各个部分中分配各自所承担的风险、功能和拥有的资产等是很难判断的,因而并没有绕开确定归属这一难题。第二,由于数字经济相较于传统经济有很大的区别,要想找到相同或相近的交易非常困难,可比性的缺失将导致 OECD 的方案很难实施。可见,如何解决数字经济下的利润归属难题仍需进一步的探究。

第二节 数字经济国际税收变革中的全球治理机制探索

面对数字经济对国际税收治理提出的严峻挑战,国际社会积极努力做出改革尝试,提出了一系列创新理念和规则方案。尽管这些理念和方案比较分散和具化,但是我们仍然能够从中发现对全球治理机制进一步完善和深化的启示。

一 数字经济背景下国际税收规则变革的初步依据

数字经济在推动跨国贸易、促进资本流通等方面发挥积极作用的同时,却给传统经济形态带来了诸多难题,特别是对传统的国际税收规则造成了巨大的冲击。例如,数字经济创造的价值难以捕获,使得对国际税收的征管和税收政策的调整面临障碍;常设机构等传统的国际税收概念不能完全适应数字经济形态下跨境税收需求等。因此在传统的国际税收规则失序的背景下,亟须在全球视角下构建国际税收新秩序。在世界各国对国际税收规则未达成整体共识之时，部分国家从本国的利益出发，纷纷制定了单边数字服务税政策，以保障本国的税收收入，但不可避免的是各国对数字企业的差异化征税政策将导致出现重复征税的问题，进而影响数字经济的发展。基于此，经合组织于2019年提出了双支柱方案，随后对该方案公开征询意见，以期重新划分数字经济形态下的国际税收权益并解决数字经济下税基严重侵蚀的问题。其中，支柱一重点关注修订关联原则和利润分配原则，在这一支柱下，共包含三项提案，分别为《用户参与提案》、《营销型无形资产提案》及《显著数字存在提案》；支柱二重点关注避免有害税收竞争，确保跨国企业的利润受到最低税率约束的问题，引入了彼此相关的"所得纳入规则"及保护市场国利益的"征税不足支付规则"这两大核心规则，由于二者均包含了最低税率要素，故在实践中常被称为《全球最低税提案》。[①]

（一）《用户参与提案》

在数字经济迅猛发展的背景下，消费群体的用户数据对经济价值的创造具有引领性的作用，已经成为价值创

---

① 朱炎生.经合组织数字经济税收规则最新提案国家间利益博弈分析[J].国际税收，2019（03）.

造链条中的核心要素，任何经营模式的企业都离不开对用户数据的收集、利用、分析。比如用户在使用产品或享受服务时输入相关用户数据，企业根据每一用户输入的数据进行整合分析从而向用户定向推送广告以实现增加平台流量及吸引消费者的目的。数字经济商业模式下，企业与用户的交互性逐步提高，用户数据无论是对于企业消费战略的制定，还是对于企业的生产经营都具有显著的贡献，已然成为企业生产经营的关键因素之一。在该背景下，《用户参与提案》认为，用户参与是数字企业获取利润的重要来源，是价值创造的关键要素，而且对于社交媒体、搜索引擎、在线销售平台这三种数字化商业模式的价值贡献度尤为突出。因此《用户参与提案》主张放弃现有的国际税收规则中的关联原则，由于数字经济无形性、虚拟性的特点，不应再像传统国际税收规则那样以物理存在与否作为判定是否属于常设机构的标准。其次，在确定利润归属时，《用户参与提案》还主张不应再坚持现有的国际税收规则中的转让定价独立交易原则，应超越该原则转而寻求一种剩余利润分配法。剩余利润分配法将企业的经营活动划分为一般经营活动及基于用户数据进行价值创造的非常规经营活动，对于一般经营活动所创造的利润适用传统的利润归属方法，对于基于用户数据进行价值创造所产生的非常规利润，按照现行转让定价方法或其他替代方法确定应归属于新征税权的范围,并将归属于新征税权的非常规利润运用相关方法分配给相关市场管辖区。由此可见,对于非常规利润,不能全部将其归属于市场国或用户国,而是应借助用户数据等价值创造因素,确定与用户参与相关的、可归属于用户所在市场国的范围,进而按照业务收入或利润贡献等指标,确定归属于不同市场管辖国的利润范围。但《用户参与提案》的目标群体仅包括对用户参与价值创造做出重大贡献的社交媒体平台、搜索引擎以及在线销售平台等高度数字化企业,对于传统经济形态下的普通企业,《用户参与提案》仍主张适用原来的利润分配原则和关联原则。同时,为了减轻税收征管和纳税合规遵从成本,《用户参与提案》还设置了业务规模的阈值,将该提案的适用范围进一步缩小至业务规模超过一定标准的超大型企业。

(二)《营销型无形资产提案》

《营销型无形资产提案》认为,企业在销售环节存在的无形资产和产品与市场国之间具有内在的功能上的联系,其依据是相较于传统经济形态下资本、劳动力是价值创造的重要来源,数字经济形态下消费者、市场等需求因素对于经济价值的创造作用更为凸显,因此只有与消费者偏好相符、能够满足消费者需求的无形资产才具有为企业创造利润的可能性。除此之外，用户数据等无形资产均来源于市场国的用户活动，因此可以将基于用户数据等的无形资产产生的利润视为在市场国产生的利润。基于该依据，《营销型无形资产提案》对于适用范围并没有做相关限制，其主张不论跨国企业在关联原则下是否在市场国设立了物理存在，只要跨国企业在市场国形成营销型无形资产，该跨国企业就应在市场国纳税。由此可知，《营销型无形资产提案》同《用户参与提案》相同，同样主张放弃经济关联原则和独立交易原则。而且该提案同样主张对现有的国际税收规则中的转让定价规则和税收协定规则进行修正，在将企业销售环节存在的无形资产及其与之有关的风险归属于市场国的同时，将营销型无形资产作为一种利润分配要素，从而使市场国有权以跨国企业在销售环节存在的无形资产及其与之有关的风险为基础，对其非常规利润进行征税，市场国由此实现了对高度数字化企业的征税权。[①] 至于企业的其他利润，则根据现有的国际税收规则中的转让定价独立交易原则在跨国企业集团的成员之间分配。而对于征税权分配方法，《营销型无形资产提案》提供了两种选择：一是确定"营销型无形资产"的范围，并

[①] 朱炎生.经合组织数字经济税收规则最新提案国家间利益博弈分析[J].国际税收，2019（03）.

根据其对企业利润的贡献度，确定应纳税金额并将其分配给市场国。二是修正剩余利润分配法并加以利用，在企业的剩余利润中，确定"营销型无形资产"创造的利润数额，并根据各国在跨国企业数字业务收入中的占比或销售额这样的商定比例，将可归属于"营销型无形资产"的利润分配给各个市场国。

（三）《显著数字存在提案》

传统经济的商业模式大多为固定的、不可移动的，远不需要过多的资本和人员流动，纳税义务人与生产国有着牢不可破的关系，所以传统的国际税收规则选择将物理存在作为关联因素，但是，随着数字经济在全球范围的蓬勃发展，现行经济形态的无形性、灵活性愈发凸显，企业无须在市场国建立物理存在，即可正常地开展生产经营活动从而获得利润。在此背景下，《显著数字存在提案》主张，只要存在可以证明跨国企业与市场国保持着稳定的目的性互动关系的要素，即可认为该企业在该市场国具有"显著数字存在"，就应在该市场国纳税。也就是说，只要可以证明产生利润的某项企业业务活动与该显著数字存在有具体联系，该市场国就有权对该业务活动所得进行征税。判断"显著数字存在"的标准包括但不限于通过线上线下为吸引客户而进行的持续营销活动、存在用户基础和相关数据等。对于征税权分配方法，《显著数字存在提案》与《用户参与提案》及《营销型无形资产提案》不同，其主张适用"部分分配法"。即在确定企业可分割税基的基础上，按照不同的分配因素及分配权重对企业的利润进行划分并确定利润归属。其中，为划分利润归属，确定企业的应税税基，需要确定企业的利润率，该利润率应使用集团整体利润率，也就是以企业的全球利润为准。此时可以制定、评估适用部分分配法的非居民实体或集团的利润额的计算方法。针对分配因素，部分分配法兼顾了供应与需求对经济价值创造的贡献，全面考量了利润分配影响因素，其中不仅包括人员、资产等传统经济形态下的重要价值贡献因素，还包括销售额、用户等代表需求贡献度的因素。虽然部分分配法以企业的全球利润率来确定应税税基并不尽善尽美，但其无须划分企业的常规利润与非常规利润，即可按照利润分配公式确定利润归属，可以省略收集跨国企业在不同国家利润情况的烦琐步骤，减轻税收核查的成本及负担，具有很强的可操作性，对于新兴经济体而言更具有可行性。

（四）《全球最低税提案》

数字经济的虚拟性、可移动性特点使得传统经济形态下纳税人与居民国牢不可破的关系被打破，一方面，纳税义务人可以在所属居民国之外的市场国进行经营获取利润，另一方面可以利用税收管辖规则的不完善避税。[①]甚至在世界各地分别进行生产经营的跨国企业，只需在税率很低、甚至是完全免征税款的国家或地区设定税收居民身份，就可实现规避税收的目的。在该背景下，为严厉打击数字经济领域的逃税、避税行为，防止税基遭受侵蚀，OECD发布的支柱二方案包含了《全球最低税提案》，该提案也被称为《全球反税基侵蚀提案》（Global Anti-Base Erosion Proposal，GloBE）。具体可以将其解释为以下两种含义。其一为设置"全球最低税率"（Global Minimum Tax），以此来保障跨国企业物理存在所在地的税收权益。当跨国企业境外来源利润的有效税率低于政治上商定的最低税率时，对其进行补偿性征税，即征收补偿税。当有效税率低于最低税率时，需要审查部分或全部低税利润是否符合某些人力资源和有形资产投资的常规回报的资格，对于不符合的情况不适用最低税率。在经过这样排除适用后，最终决定征收的补偿税金额。其二是为保护市场国的税收权益，当跨国企业的有效税率低于政治上商定的最低税率时，市场国可以禁止跨国企业扣除成本，从而扩大税

[①] 崔虹.拨开迷雾：数字经济下税收管辖分配规则三重挑战的应对[J].国际经济法学刊，2020（04）.

基、增加跨国企业的应税金额。另外，对于补偿税而言，可采纳以下两种规则：赋予母公司缴纳补偿税义务的所得纳入规则、对产生集团内部支付的公司征收税款的征税不足支付规则。[1]

二 数字经济背景下国际税收机制变革的基本趋势

（一）国际税收合作应从双边走向多边

随着互联网和信息技术的飞跃发展，以"世界多极化、经济全球化、文化多样化、社会信息化"为突出特征的新的世界格局正在逐步形成。[2]而数字经济的跨越式发展在带来新业态、新体制、新商业模式，对生产生活各个方面进行变革的同时，也使得金融、投资、税收等方面的全球性问题日益突出。[3]所以为解决这些问题，各个主权国家及国际组织应联合起来，统筹协调国际行动，积极实现合作

---

[1] 约阿希姆·恩利施，刘奇超，沈涛，肖畅，任雪丽.国际有效最低税：对全球反税基侵蚀提案（支柱二）的分析[J/OL].海关与经贸研究.[2021-06-29]. http://kns.cnki.net/kcms/detail/31.2093.f.20210628.1319.002.html.
[2] 邓力平.百年未有之大变局下的中国国际税收研究[J].国际税收，2020（02）.
[3] 马述忠，郭继文.数字经济时代的全球经济治理：影响解构、特征刻画与取向选择[J].改革，2020（11）.

和共治，共同构建适应数字经济形态的全球治理体制机制，推动世界经济朝着包容、可持续的方向发展，进一步完善世界经济格局。而税收制度作为保障各国税收秩序的重要制度，与各国的政治、经济、文化、社会信息密不可分，不同政治、经济、文化、社会背景的国家，税收制度有差异，对同一经济行为的处理方式也存在差异，各国税收制度的多元化、差异化让全球性市场经济的发展处于困境，此时就需要加强国际税收合作，积极关注国际税收秩序的变动。在国际税收治理由传统型走向现代化的过程中，作为税收治理一部分的税收合作也逐渐呈现新的特点。传统经济形态下，国际税收合作大多以签订双边税收协定的双边合作模式为主。但在大变革时代，经济全球化盛行，税收治理也朝着全球化深入发展，有学者将全球税收治理看作国际税收治理发展到新阶段的产物，认为无论是税收还是税制都是全球性问题，国际治理既需要全球性的税收制度与征管制度，也需要更强的国际法意识。[①]因此在强调全球税收治理的背景下，原本的国家间的双边税收治理问题日渐显露，其中跨国公司利用传统国际税收规则的漏洞而实行避税的问题尤为严重，而双边税收合作难以发挥作用。

---

① 罗秦.国际税收治理从双边到多边的演进：新格局、新挑战及新趋势[J].国际税收，2021（01）.

此时应打破传统的以在居民国与来源国之间签订税收协定为主的双边合作模式，从双边走向多边，由多边国家共同参与，才有利于形成良好、可持续发展的国际税收秩序。相较于传统的双边治理，多边国际税收治理呈现如下几个特征。其一，国际组织在国际税收治理中的作用愈发凸显，比如G20峰会多次将税收议题作为重要主题，积极倡导对国际税收治理秩序的改善。其二，国际税收治理的重心转为重建国际税收新秩序。传统经济形态下，国际税收治理的主要内容为避免双重征税，但在数字经济蓬勃发展的背景下，国际税收治理的核心内容已转变为严厉打击避税，防范双重不征税，从而维护税收的公平正义，努力保障各国的税收权益。其三，国际税收的治理机制在不断探索中，传统的国际税收治理机制以国际的双边税收协定为主，但这一单一治理机制已不能解决数字经济背景下国际税收产生的新问题，因此亟须构建新阶段下的国际税收治理机制，为此以经合组织为代表的国际组织纷纷出台以构建国际税收新规则为目的的文件或报告，虽然各国对此尚未达成共识，但是相关探索性文件的出台确实在引导国际税收秩序朝着透明、公平、可持续的方向发展。

（二）以人类命运共同体意识重构国际税收新秩序

新的世界格局的特点之一是世界多极化，因此在重构国际税收规则之时，应注重从国际政治视角来聚焦国际税收关系。以美国为代表的发达国家是传统国际税收规则制定的主导者，无论是规则的拟定还是表决权的行使，发达国家都占据垄断地位，而发展中国家只能被动地接受既有的国际税收规则。国际税收规则的制定体现着主权国家利益的斗争，所以以发达国家为主导制定的传统国际税收规则，更多的是维护发达国家的税收利益。但随着世界格局朝着多极化方向发展，西方发达国家经济实力的衰退及发展中国家、新兴经济体经济实力的上升，使得新兴经济体在全球经济治理中的作用愈发突出，体现在国际税收中就是其在税收规则的制定上拥有相较于以往更大的话语权。当前国际税收呈现合作与竞争并存的格局，各国既在税收利益分配时存在竞争，又针对反对利润转移和侵蚀税基、避免恶性税收竞争和双重征税展开合作。而且当前国际税收竞争与合作的主体已不再仅仅是独立的主权国家，发达国家与发展中国家之间、新兴经济体之间同样存在着税收利益的争夺。所以为实现发达国家与新兴经济体税收利益的协调及平衡，亟须对由发达国家为主导制定的传统国际税收规则进行重构。国际税收规则的制定过程也是各国利益再分配的过程，因此应在新的世界格局逐步形成的背景下，基于人类命运共同体的意识重构国际税收新秩序，在各国的税收规则中寻求最大公约数，基于各国普遍认可的价值制定基础的国际税收规则，以为全球经济的包容、可持续发展提供制度保障。

在大变局时代，在国际税收规则的调整中，政治因素已经优先于经济因素。所以对于国际税收规则的重建，从政治层面来说，应首先增进不同国家之间的政治互信，促进各国政府在本着信赖原则的基础上对税收进行合作共治，以期实现共赢目标，共享发展红利并推动国际税收秩序逐步实现公平正义并走向现实均衡。其次，在税收规则的制定上，各国政府应以包容、开放、全面的态度看待税收问题，不应仅从本国利益出发，谋求仅对本国有利的税收规则，而是应综合考量税收规则对不同经济体的利弊，同世界各国共同探讨有利于构建国际税收治理秩序的税收规则。从经济层面来说，首先应顺应经济全球化的浪潮，密切关注国际税收协调的新表现形式，确定新的常设机构利润归属方法等。其次在税收征管领域也应积极贯彻人类命运共同体的精神，推动税收征管技术方面的互助协作，利用信息技术等手段加强各国税收征管机构之间的信息共享，提升税收征管胜任能力，[1] 推动税收征管向数字化方向转型，以维护国际税收秩序。

---

[1] 刘建徽，周志波.经济数字化与全球税收治理：背景、困境与对策[J].宏观经济研究，2020（06）.

（三）以开放的视角重新明确政府的定位

政府作为国家进行统治和社会管理的机关，其经济职能包括市场监管及提供公共服务。就市场监管而言，政府与市场的角色定位并不是互相排斥的矛盾对立关系，而是相辅相成的补充关系，政府通过税收征管实现对资源的再分配，并通过对经济资源征税来维持政府的运转，从而更好地实现提供公共服务的政府职能。就提供公共服务而言，政府通过提供就业机会，保障教育、养老、医疗，提供基础设施等公共服务参与社会经济价值创造，虽然在经济价值创造的过程中，存在高喊"政府失灵""有限政府"的声音，但从未有人否定过政府在经济价值创造过程中的贡献。这意味着在社会的整体运转中，政府已经成为参与价值创造的生产单位。而政府在提供公共服务、市场监管等职能中所体现的贡献也就构成了政府征税权的基础。在大变革时代，重构国际税收规则，应打破西方市场的自由化意识，意识到政府在社会财富创造过程中的重要作用，认识到政府与私人部门之间的关系实际就是生产要素与中间产品的交换关系，从而在立足政府贡献的基础上，寻求最大公约数，推动国际税收新秩序的建立。[①]

---

① 曹明星，杜建伟. 寻求重构国际税收秩序的最大公约数 [N]. 中国税务报，2016-09-07（B01）.

第二章
数字经济国际税收治理变革的理论创新

通过对数字经济国际税收治理变革战略背景与机制探索的总体梳理,新时代的国际税收治理研究亟须基础理论的创新,才能够进一步确立改革的战略路径和政策框架。由此,我们一方面要在国家层面对市场经济中的国家税收依据理论进行再思考,从政府贡献视角补全可比交易全景,重新论证国家/政府税收的正当性及其边界;另一方面在国际层面考虑跨境交易中的国际税收管辖权再分配,在国际贸易和国际投资等环节创新利润生成和分配机制,平衡生产国和市场国(原来的居民国和来源国)的税收利益和权利。

第一节 政府贡献与市场经济中的
国家税收依据再思考

在国家层面,企业的私有价值创造与国家的公共价值创造是共生的,市场交易框架的多层次性能够解释,企业和国家的价值创造统一于交换中商品价值的总体成本和剩余价值上。

一 政府与价值创造的关系

（一）政府的生产角色

若以劳动价值论去探寻价值创造的源泉，并由此去理解私人产品与公共产品的关系、政府收入与社会财富的关系、征税与纳税的关系，与纯私人视角是截然不同的。在社会生产与再生产过程中，公共产品与私人产品生产之间不再是纯粹割裂的，两者在经济意义上存在一种联系，公共产品服务于私人产品。另外，私人产品也服务于公共产品，对公共产品的提供起到促进作用。基于此，我们认为私人产品与公共产品互相服务、互为生产要素、互为中间产品、互为价值交换。总而言之，私人产品的生产消耗了公共产品，即私人产品中蕴含着私人要素与公共要素，从而私人产品的生产过程中不能忽视公共部门的价值贡献。

（二）政府与价值创造

从现实实践来说，生产、分配、交换、消费四个环节均离不开政府（公共部门）的身影。比如这四个环节均需要一个良好的市场环境，需要稳定的市场秩序与健全的法律制度，这些都需要政府去维护与建立。各国政府部门执政能力与服务水平有所差异，且由于制度等因素的存在，在产品生产、分配、交换、消费环节中难免出现"政府失灵""市场失灵""有限政府"的问题，但是大家的争论焦点一直是围绕着政府的贡献价值大小展开，而不是政府是否有价值贡献，人们对政府贡献从未有过质疑，对政府贡献一直持肯定的态度。

在价值创造过程中，市场主体具有"理性人"属性，政府亦具有"理性人"属性，二者共同参与社会财富的创造过程。只不过在这个过程中，市场主体直接参与价值创造，而政府参与价值创造的过程相对隐蔽，没有市场主体的参与那么直观。政府是以基础设施、市场制度、社会管理，甚至是以国防、教育资源等各种形式参与社会生产与价值创造，因此我们可以认为社会价值创造既是政府收入之源，更离不开政府的贡献，政府贡献是联通社会财富创造与政府收入的桥梁。[①]事实上，从经济学视角来看，私人产品、公共产品以及社会财富之间的逻辑关系是十分清晰的，即社会财富由私人产品与公共产品组合构成。但是当把问题细化时，因各国不同的政治制度、经济制度有所

---

① 曹明星，杜建伟.政府贡献：重构国际税收秩序的最大公约数[J].国际税收，2016（10）.

差异，各国政府的生产角色也表现得略有差异。已有研究对税收的本质认识出现了巨大的偏差，基本可以分为两大阵营，一部分人认为税收是政府凭借其政治权力对社会财富的强制分配与暴力掠夺，再分配的过程并无经济逻辑可言，简单粗暴；而另外一部分人认为税收的本质是一个价值交换的过程，政府与私人部门在价值创造过程中均投入了一定的生产要素，公共部门与私人部门理应共享价值创造的果实。

（三）税收征税权基础：政府贡献

从经济学角度出发，同私人部门一样，公共部门也具有"理性人"属性，也是逐利的，市场主体与政府部门均参与了产品的价值创造过程，市场主体与政府部门在经济意义上并无实质差别，都属于要素投入者。因此本书认为公共产品实际上是作为一种生产要素，与私人产品一同进入社会财富的价值创造过程中，所以政府部门理应参与到社会财富的分配中，对于其付出理应享有应得部分的税收补偿。顺着这个逻辑思路，政府与私人部门之间并不是传统认为的对立关系，恰恰相反，政府与私人部门是互利共赢的要素投资者，类似"股东"关系，是一种"要素共投、利益共享"的合作关系，这一点对于我们理解税收本质与征税权基础有着巨大的作用与意义。

由前文所述，税收是私人部门对消耗公共产品的补偿和相应的利益分享，征税并非政府凭借政治权力强制性掠夺私人部门的利益与财富，而是政府正当权益的行使，因此本书认为政府贡献是征税权的基础。无论是居民国还是市场国，其征税权均是基于价值创造过程占用了一定的公共资源，消耗了一定的公共产品。例如，企业在市场国享受了其基础设施、行政管理、市场监管等，居民国的企业更是如此，市场国与居民国能对企业征收税收的逻辑起点就在于此，国际税收的征收权划分也是基于政府贡献，基于所享受的公共服务。所以，将价值创造论与政府贡献放在一起讨论，不难发现政府贡献对价值创造的作用巨大，难以忽视政府的贡献；但是，同时我们也发现政府贡献的价值量难以衡量，因为就单个个体而言，其承担的税负水平与实际享受到的公共资源不一定是等量的，可能并不匹配。

二　价值创造与利益分配错位

（一）政府贡献与价值创造难以衡量

将价值创造论与政府贡献放在一起讨论，虽然前文已经论述了政府贡献在社会生产与价值创造中的重要性与不可或缺，但是随之而来的一个问题是，政府贡献的价值是多少？我们发现政府贡献的价值是难以衡量的。首先，公共产品存在正外部性，即公共产品具有非排他性与非竞争性，边际成本很低且所有微观主体都可以占用或消耗公共产品；其次，公共产品供给与微观主体的税负之间不符合独立交易原则；最后，公共产品的供给并无市场公允价格可供参考，也没有可比对象。因此，就企业微观主体而言，其享受的政府服务是难以度量的。政府根据社会整体消耗的公共服务与资源情况，制定一个既符合市场发展规律又能筹集到一定财政收入的税率水平，对社会财富进行分配，这就导致单个个体负担的税收总额与其所享受到的公共服务与公共资源可能不一定是等量的，政府就自己投入的公共要素与所得税收利益也可能并不匹配，即存在价值创造与利益分配错位的情形。

（二）税基侵蚀与利润转移加剧分配失衡

随着新自由主义的发展，资本在全球范围的自由流动加速，跨国企业的寡头垄断地位不断巩固加强，资本的逐利特性也不断展现出来，导致世界各国的税收主权受到威胁与侵犯，利润转移使得大量应征税款流失，引起国际税收领域的秩序失衡与征管争端问题。[1]由于世界很多国家

---

[1] 曹明星，杜建伟.政府贡献：重构国际税收秩序的最大公约数[J].国际税收，2016（10）.

的税法体系并不完善、国际税收协定也存在诸多漏洞，国际税收管辖权的规定并不清晰，在税权划分上存在一些漏洞，跨国公司利用成本分摊协议、资本弱化、转让定价漏洞以及滥用税收协定、设立中介控股公司等各种手段进行逃避税活动，从而实现利润转移，侵蚀了税收主权国家的税基。税基侵蚀与利润转移，实际上背离了劳动创造价值是唯一源泉这一基本思想，将利润分配与实际经营活动分离开来，导致的直接后果是企业享受了政府提供的公共服务，但是政府不能基于自己提供的公共服务参与利润分配，无法行使或仅能部分行使其应有的征税权。

（三）价值创造与利益分配错位问题日益凸显

价值创造与利益分配错位，导致对政府贡献的税收补偿是远远不足的。当政府贡献的税收补偿长期不能得到充分弥补时，政府提供公共服务的质量与效率也将大幅下降，这对于经济的整体稳定发展会产生不利影响。因此，随着2008年国际金融危机的爆发以及欧美发达国家（地区）的经济发展停滞不前，欧美国家（地区）的债务危机日益严重，财政赤字率大幅增加，对提升政府收入的激励加大，这使政府贡献的税收补偿不足问题日益凸显，利益错配问题也被提上议程，税基侵蚀与利润转移（BEPS）行动计划应运而生。

资本的逐利属性驱使跨国公司热衷于利用国际税收

协定以及市场国、生产国的税法漏洞，将利润转移至避税地区以达到降低企业总体税负水平的目的，一些国家的税基遭受巨大的侵蚀。BEPS 行动计划明确了"产品或服务的价值大部分来自上游活动或下游活动末端发生作用的阶段"的价值创造论，但是在全球价值链中，不等价交换使得剩余价值由外围向中心国家转移，所体现的就是跨国公司转移了政府贡献所应得的税收补偿，即政府贡献与税收补偿之间的矛盾。虽然 BEPS 行动计划在全球国际税收征管合作中作用巨大，反避税机制与制度日益健全，反避税合作形式日益多样化，反避税措施更加有效且具有针对性，但是 BEPS 行动计划也有一些局限性，如国际合作有待进一步深化，国际偷逃税活动仍旧屡禁不止，不能从根本上改善税基侵蚀与利润转移所导致的政府贡献的价值创造与利益分配错位问题。

三　现有利益分配规则的困境[①]

（一）独立交易原则与全球公式分配法的缺陷

对于税基侵蚀与利润转移所造成的价值创造与利益分

[①] 杜建伟，曹明星.国际税收治理变革的几个基本问题探讨——数字经济下的税收权力、价值创造、公私交换与税基确定 [J].国际税收，2021（01）.

配错位问题，目前理论上有"独立交易原则"和"全球公式分配法"两种解决办法。"独立交易原则"下的转让定价调整方法可以分为以价格为基础和以利润为基础的两大类转让定价调整方法，包括成本加成法、再销售价格法、交易净利润法、可比非受控价格法以及利润分割法。一般情况下，"独立交易原则"的调整方法是寻找一个类似的独立可比对象与可比交易，以其为基础对非独立交易进行调整。"全球公式分配法"是依据跨国集团内各关联企业之间的营业额、成本费用、资产总额、工资水平等要素，按照既定的公式与比例在各个企业之间进行分配，计算各自的应纳税所得额，各自在所在国纳税。

就"独立交易原则"下的调整方法而言，其解决税基侵蚀与利润转移的方法是通过对交易对价进行调整，使得非独立交易价格与独立交易价格保持一致，从而减少税源的流失，实现对政府贡献的利益补偿。一般而言，只有在生产要素保持自由流动、市场充分竞争的条件下，交易才可能实现独立且等价。事实上，与其他生产要素不同，作为价值创造的源泉，劳动力这一生产要素尤为特殊。资本、技术等生产要素可以根据各国供需情况在国家间自由流动，而劳动力却因为政治、语言等多方面原因难以在各国之间自由流动，在现实中很难找到一个满足条件的可比交易，因此使用"独立交易原则"可能陷入关联交易大量存在而可比的"独立"交易却难以找到的尴尬境地。不仅如此，即使冲破种种限制条件，在国家间找到了独立可比交易，但是在剩余价值从外围流向中心的情况下，所谓"独立"交易往往因为处于"外围"国家而失去正义基础，严格意义上并不符合要求。

就"全球公式分配法"而言，其解决税基侵蚀与利润转移的方法并非通过对单项交易进行逐笔调整，而是综合集团内各个企业的营业额、成本费用、资产总额、工资水平等要素水平，将总利润在各个企业间进行分配。"全球公式分配法"以要素价值论为基础，因此遮盖了劳动力作为价值源泉的唯一性特征。

此外，值得注意的是，税收分配作为政府贡献补偿的一种形式，既受制于经济发展水平，也受制于产权结构与政府收入结构的影响，这就意味着国际税收分配不能单纯从税收层面看待税收，还要从经济发展阶段、产权结构等方面看待税收分配问题。

（二）数字经济发展给跨国企业避税创造了便利

随着数字经济时代的来临，大数据、云计算、网络支付、区块链等新兴技术不断出现与发展，商业模式也发生巨大变化。从国际税收角度来看，数字经济并不依赖于传统的显著数字存在或物理的实体存在，这也就意味着来源国无征税权，对来源于本国的所得无法征税，这给国际税收带来了巨大的挑战。数字经济对国际税收带来严峻挑战的根本原因在于，国际税收管辖权设置中存在着先天缺陷，在没有物理实体存在的情况下，无法提供一个公平有效的征税权划分框架与征收机制。在数字经济时代，全球价值链中包括互联网平台、虚拟商店、网上支付等新的商业交易模式，呈现高流动性、高数据化、极度依赖无形资产、强调用户参与等特征，这些特征使得交易更加隐蔽与不可追踪，加大了国际税收征管工作的难度与复杂性，为跨国企业进行利润转移与逃税避税活动提供了便利，加剧了跨国企业对市场国的税基侵蚀。

在国际税收的演变中，"经济关联原则"一直扮演着国际税收权划分的角色。但是随着数字经济的到来，商业交易由线下改为线上进行，国际社会曾经坚持的"利润应在经济活动发生地和价值创造地课税"的基本原则受到巨大的冲击。首先，国际税收征税的经济关联原则在缺乏物理实体存在的情况下，难以划分各国的税收管辖权；其次，以数据、信息为载体的标的，其价值难以准确衡量，现实中也很难找到一个可比的交易对象，因此不能合理确定税基，此外，数字经济下甚至对国际税收关于征税主体、征税对象、征税方式乃至税种性质均产生重大疑问，基于此，我们认为现有国际税收征税权划分规则受到了严重挑战。

四 以政府贡献重构国际税收新秩序

综上所述,"独立交易原则"和"全球公式分配法"都存在一定的缺陷,且随着数字经济时代的到来,税基侵蚀与利润转移导致价值创造与利益分配错位问题不断加剧,现有国际税收征税权划分规则受到严重挑战。国际社会需要立足新的视角,在"独立交易原则"和"全球公式分配法"之外,探索一个新的国际税收利益划分规则,重新构建国际税收秩序。

政府提供公共服务与公共资源以参与价值创造过程,因此价值创造完成后应当给予政府税收形式的要素投入补偿。由此可见,国际税收利益的划分,实际上是以对政府贡献充分补偿为基础的征税权的划分,试图实现政府贡献的价值创造与利益分配相匹配的目标。基于此,国际税收新秩序可以从政府贡献角度出发,从价值交换理论层面出发,解决无物理实体存在而不能课税的现实问题,回归税收的强制性特征,遵循强制性原则,绕过无实体常设机构不可征税的困境与尴尬局面。基于这个新视角与新逻辑,寻找最大公约数,以政府贡献重新构建国际税收秩序,[①] 紧紧围绕政府贡献—价值创造—政府

[①] 曹明星,杜建伟. 寻求重构国际税收秩序的最大公约数 [N]. 中国税务报,2016-09-07(B01).

贡献补偿这条主线，[①]构建"政府贡献成本"和"政府贡献成本节约"两个概念，重新对国际税收利益进行分配，以期能够解决政府部门与跨国企业、一般国家与避税地国家、中心国家与外围国家之间的关系。

第二节　供需利润与跨境交易中的国际税收管辖权再分配

从全球层面看国际贸易和投资领域，生产国的价值创造和市场国的价值创造是相辅相成的，市场国形成使用和消费能力的价值创造不能被货币支付所遮蔽，而是需要还原为不同生产者之间的价值交换，才能够共享利润和税基，从而从国家和世界两个维度发现和还原国际税收治理新理念的理论形成轨迹。

一　国际税收管辖权分配的理论依据

（一）关联度与市场国征税权的本质

从本质而言，数字税改（即数字经济国际税收改革）

[①] 曹明星，杜建伟. 私人交换＋公私交换：从政府贡献视角补全可比交易全景 [J]. 税务研究，2020（07）.

起始于"市场国"概念的形成和市场国"新型"征税权的确立,数字经济税收需要有自己的正当依据和基本原则。基于 BEPS 行动计划框架建立的"利润应在经济活动发生地和价值创造地征税"的理念,其实就是关联度的原型。但是在数字经济条件下,无形资产的应用、无实体存在的经营、无直接对价的交换等,使得业务无法遵循传统的以生产国或常设机构征税权为基础的国际税收规则,来直接给予市场国征税权(尤其是所得税征税权)。数字化企业在各个国家经营,但政府无法在传统税收规则下确定征税对象,数字经济的发展让传统的税收规则面临着失灵的风险。然而,如果我们撇开现象,还原跨境交易的本质,也许就可以看清其真相。其实关联度问题才是国际税收管辖权的起点,关联度不应仅是方案中的一个技术性连接点,它实际上体现了征税权的正当性,决定了征税主体、对象、范围与标准。然而,当前的现状是,OECD 试图以简单实惠的技术问题的解决略过原则性和正当性的争议,短平快地解决问题。然而,国际税收应该是以共识为基础的规则体系,一旦偏离"以原则为基础"(principle-based)的前提条件,很可能会因为各方理念无法一致而争议不断,在实践时也难以达到应有的协调效果,这将与规则的目的相悖。由此,重新理清数字税改的基本理念和原则至关重要。

在经济活动中，生产者和消费者相伴相生，生产者和消费者之间的交易实际上是生产者 A 和生产者 B 之间交换使用价值，所谓的消费者，只是先前的生产者（或者未来的生产者）。在认识到交易是生产者之间价值交换的基础上，再还原二者在各国的纳税义务及税基分割问题。如果我们承认国家征税是基于政府贡献而进行的成本补偿和收益分享，那么显然生产者 A 和生产者 B 将因为提供不同的使用价值而创造出交换价值，而分别就其生产使用价值的成本和交换价值中的利润，对各自的国家承担消费税和所得税的纳税义务，这样就解决了生产者 B 也就是消费者所在市场国征税权的依据问题。

在劳动分工和比较优势的背景下，我们假设在以货易货的情形下（以下简称"情形一"），A 国生产者 A 提供产品或者服务 X 的不含税成本为 80 元（如果提供 Y 则是 90 元），B 国生产者 B 提供产品或者服务 Y 的不含税成本为 80 元（如果提供 X 则是 90 元），双方就 A 提供 X 和 B 提供 Y 达成交易，在劳动分工和比较优势的背景下，双方各有使用价值获得和交换价值增益，A 国和 B 国政府也相应地对生产者 A 和生产者 B 征收公共成本补偿税和收益分享税。虽然是各自征税，但是其实已经存在就一个交易产生的总剩余的分割和重复征税问题。

在信用货币时代，在以货币作为交易联结的情况下

（以下简称"情形二"），假设双方达成的交易价格为85元，由于消费者B（情形一中的生产者B）是以货币85元替换、延展并遮断了生产者B以成本80元的使用价值Y得到生产者A成本80元的使用价值X的环节，并只能通过货币联结的方式将双方的交换剩余集中于生产者A得到的5元，这个数值实际上也体现了生产者B的部分剩余，于是A国和B国只能通过合适的方式进行交易情景还原，才能确定各自的征税权。

而如果情形二得以还原到情形一，生产者B势必尽可能地以其成本80元的Y从生产者A得到交换价值85元，两国就此贸易才能达到平衡和可持续，如此B国的消费税和所得税的全部计税逻辑是完整的；但在实践中我们看到的通常是，B国只以货币价值85元作为X的进口成本征收消费税，未计征所得税。多收了5元税基的消费税但没有考虑在初始情形一中相互比较优势下产生的5元（90-85）消费者B/生产者B剩余，从而损失了相应税基的所得税，而且在供给自动创造需求的短缺经济时代，利润和税基会向生产要素更为优势的一方偏移，造成由市场格局的差异导致的损失增加。这才是市场国失去所得税征税权的由来，以及国际税收征税权失衡的本源，也是本书谈及的国际税收传统实践中错误配置跨境贸易和跨境投资国际税收管辖权的根源。

（二）跨境交易剩余分割理论的历史再还原

为了给市场国新型征税权寻找理论依据，OCED 数字税改方案中提出了"使用者（和消费者）与生产者共同创造价值"的观点。方案中提出的新价值创造理论至少面临三方面的问题。一是，虽然少数自动数字化服务的市场平台因为使用者的参与而生成一种"产消者"（prosumer）主体，从而形成部分价值创造和价值贡献，但是对于大多数的产业数字化经济如面向消费者业务而言，人们观察到的依然是交易中的买卖双方，其中作为消费者的买方其价值创造与贡献仍然存疑，即使存在也只应当从市场国自身税基的角度进行观察，市场国自然也就无从产生所谓的针对生产者的所得税征税权，此时的价值创造理论不能对其提供正当性支持。二是，既然提供消费者业务的数字企业应当向市场国分配所得税税基，等于承认了消费者和市场国在数字交易中的价值创造，那难道数字化之前跨境交易中的消费者就没有共同创造价值？如果照此推演下去，在所有的跨境交易中，生产国和市场国都应当分享交易所得税的征税权，这不符合实践常识。三是，如果新的价值创造理论成立，市场国新征税权的正当性得以全面确立，这将挑战原有的国际税收原理，从而引起国际税收秩序的重大变化，对世界经济产生重大影响。

第二章 数字经济国际税收治理变革的理论创新

第一个问题实际上是价值创造的理论有效性问题。首先，依据前述论证，政府征税的依据在于税收是公共产品和公共服务的对价，税收的基础是政府的价值创造和贡献，而不是企业的价值创造，企业恰恰是作为价值消耗者而承担纳税义务。在这个角度上，价值创造理论既失灵了又没有失灵，失灵是因为政府不能（本质上也不是）依据企业价值创造对其征税，没有失灵是因为政府征税是一种对利润或者剩余价值的分割，其依据就是政府的价值创造，价值创造理论仍然能够从全局上和根本上提供解释和支撑。其次，对于使用者和消费者概念的打通，如前述例子描述，其价值创造在于开放经济中比较优势下不同使用价值的生产，继而形成参与跨境交易的使用和消费能力。这是其参与利润分享的依据，也是因为他们的公共价值消耗从而构成政府征税的基础。只有厘清其中的逻辑层次，才能完整把握价值创造理论。

第二个问题是市场国征税权的历史存在性问题。在国际税收管辖权分配的最初讨论中，经济学家一直在讨论"供需利润观"。一些国际税收专家指出，企业利润的来源（价值创造）中包含了市场客户创造的利润（价值），市场国有权对企业的跨境销售所得课税。但是，在20世纪20年代国际税收规则设计的时候，技术专家放弃了经济学家的"供需利润观"而采纳了"供应利润观"，即在跨国企

043

业产生的来自不同国家的营业利润，在国际税收权益分配上应当实行常设机构原则，这主要是基于在当时历史条件下销售市场国对非居民跨境营业利润行使来源地征税权课税的实际可行性考虑，并没有充足的经济原理支撑。这种做法从根本上剥夺了销售市场国在非居民企业未在其境内构成常设机构、却获得来自境内的销售利润的情况下参与分享税收利益的"权利"，也严重偏离了经济学家提出的"经济忠诚原则"（Principle of Economic Allegiance）的完整内涵要求。

更令人遗憾的是，后来 OECD 国际税收协定范本不但没有认识和纠正这一偏差，反而在此基础上，将非居民企业是否在市场国境内构成常设机构性质的物理存在，进一步曲解为一种基于"经济忠诚原则"、衡量非居民企业是否实质性参与市场国经济生活的标准，并以此确定市场国是否有权对非居民企业的跨境营业利润课税的一般政策依据。这实际上是以跨境投资中来源国是否有权参与居民国利润和税收分配的局部问题，彻底掩盖了市场国与生产国对跨境交易的交易剩余具有同等但独享的税收权的基础性问题。

第三个问题是理论还原和原则澄清后的实践接受度问题。我们必须看到，在国际税收领域，跨国企业利用税制差异和漏洞开展的激进避税，极大地侵蚀着来源国和居民国的税基，如果再加上市场国（与来源国有很大程度的重叠，但分类逻辑不同）征税权的长期缺失，将严重削弱政府提供公共服务的国家能力；在数字经济时代更加凸显的传统国际税收规则的弊端，将进一步恶化和加速由市场国征税权缺失导致的国家间消费力的不平衡和不可持续，最终导致以金融链断裂为标志的全球性经济危机。理性看待国际税收规则的创新，就必须接受和还原市场国的基础性正当征税权。尽管改革可以渐进实施，但是只有建构一个生产国和市场国利益公平、征税权平衡的国际税收规则，才是开放经济下国家经济和全球化经济健康发展的正确路径。

二　跨境交易的剩余利润分配新征税权规则

（一）适用范围的产业链和价值链考量

数字企业和传统企业在税收的征管层面存在很大的不同，数字企业若按照传统的税收规则来征税，就会承担较小的税收责任，这对传统的国际税基分割是较大的冲击，因此 OECD 提出了支柱一方案。在 OECD 的方案里，首次赋予处于数字经济产业链下游的市场国以新型的所得税征税权，但同时基于各国政府间的博弈，改革方案又将其在工业经济时代居民国和生产国的既得征税权加以保留，从而达成一种有限进步性的改革。

支柱一方案聚焦新关联度，核心在于明确两项重要内容。一是授予市场国新征税权（即金额 A），将跨国企业集团层面（或业务线层面）剩余利润的一部分确认为金额 A，按照达成共识的分配要素利用公式将金额 A 在各合格市场国之间进行分配。二是对发生在市场国境内的某些基础性营销和分销活动，按照简化的"独立交易原则"给予固定回报，也即金额 B。因此，支柱一方案的核心价值在于提出的新征税权，即在放弃传统国际税收规则的"独立实体原则"、"经济关联原则"和"独立交易原则"的基础上，以基于公式分配的方法实现向市场国的利润分配和税基分割。

事实上，"市场国"概念的形成，是以欧盟为主导的 OECD 对国际税收规则进行自我革命的产物。在工业经济阶段，欧洲很多国家长期居于产业链的上游，OECD 极力推崇的以居民国为基础的国际税收管辖权，使得欧洲国家受益颇丰。但在新经济条件下，中美（尤其是美国）数字经济发展迅速，并显著地处于世界领先地位，而欧盟总体只是居于产业链下游，无法再依据传统的居民国管辖权获取国际税收的偏向性收益。于是 OECD 创造了"市场国"概念，越过"独立交易原则"，赋予并加强了传统来源国无法得到的税收管辖权和征税权。

第二章 数字经济国际税收治理变革的理论创新

　　基于以上认知，市场国征税权的确立实际上是一种正当秩序的回归，应当适用于所有跨境交易，包括数字商品和服务交易。这样，跨境交易的国际税收管辖权得以平衡。数字经济的征税权改革应当以此原理和原则进行重塑。但是，OECD一方面在尚未达成全面共识的情况下，在有限程度上积极推动了市场国征税权的确立；另一方面又掩盖和隐藏了当前数字经济时代跨境交易征税权的平衡需求，对数字服务税进行了"圈离"，以实现对发达国家产业链和价值链既有利益的保护。

　　有专家敏锐地指出了OECD支柱一方案在利益与规则方面的逻辑脉络。首先，支柱一方案将金额A的适用范围从高度数字化的企业收窄为自动化数字服务，提出新征税权对适用金额A的企业在市场国只分配剩余利润，这是规则的逻辑起点；其次，支柱一方案从远程营销的有限风险分销商中剥离出面向消费者的业务，将远程营销的有限风险分销商的大部分收益转为范围比金额A大许多但不分行业和规模的金额B。这样，通过对适用范围行业性的排除，支柱一方案可以收到至少以下三个直接效果。一是使跨国数字巨头税负最小化。自动化数字服务使许多跨国数字企业没有进入征税范围，即便进入征税范围也仅仅需要分配剩余利润的很少一部分，而且使税负最小化。二是保护欧美国家既得利益。金额A、金额B适用范围的设计，既使西方具备优势的服务贸易受到的影响最小化，又使远程营销的有限风险分销商的架构、对外支付特许权使用费的惯例、避税地（低税国）的存在等跨国企业的既得利益得到保护。三是利用规则获得额外利益。在上述操作基础上，因为美国、欧盟是全球最大的消费市场，金额 A 中面向消费者业务的利润分配与金额 B 中基本分销活动的回报，有可能大大多于自动化数字服务分出的金额 A，欧美国家（地区）由此所获收益将超过在新征税权方面的"损失"。

基于上述分析，OECD 支柱一方案规则的设计保证了欧美国家一起获益，但忽略和侵害了广大发展中国家的利益。有鉴于此，国际社会需要推动 OECD 公平确立市场国征税权的适用范围，减少不合理的"圈定"和"圈离"，尽量实现征税权的全面公平、税制的简化统一。只有这样，才是真正积极地应对数字经济的挑战，才能更加有效地解决国际税收的基本问题。

（二）公式分配规则的税基和要素选择

2019 年国际货币基金组织（IMF）在其发表的工作报告《剩余利润分配的探讨》中，将跨国企业的利润划分为两部分：一部分是常规利润，体现在市场国从事活动与发挥功能的正常回报；另一部分是加总利润减去常规利润的剩余利润，要基于某些公式分配到市场国。但是，OECD

第二章 数字经济国际税收治理变革的理论创新

的剩余利润分配法未提及在市场国的常规回报，只提及集团剩余利润向市场国的分配，并通过一个预设的固定比例确定市场国的税基。这种设计不但偏离了国际社会对常规利润和非常规利润分配规则的理性讨论，也否定了我们之前讨论的基于交换价值达成的分别由生产国和市场国所有的税收管辖权。

OECD除了通过分配规则设定限制了征税范围外，实际上还人为地限制了剩余利润公式分配的全面适用。支柱一方案赋予拥有自动化数字服务和面向消费者业务的市场国剩余利润征税权，但是设定的分配比例为剩余利润的20%。这种设定以一种渐进的方式改革了国际税收规则，保证了市场国的征税权。但是，分配规则一方面暗含以市场国企业的价值贡献为分配依据的理念，实际上是以市场国企业争夺生产国企业剩余利润来混淆市场国政府的基础性征税权；另一方面，市场国政府的基础性征税权在很大程度上是市场国"以支定收"的自主性税收权，其公式分配理念和要素也必然不同于也不全然依赖于企业的价值创造和贡献。

总之，分配规则的设计是征税权实现的关键途径。OECD延续了之前的改革思路，试图以有限公平的改革一方面实现自己的新增税收利益，另一方面又隐藏和保护既得税收利益，最大程度地限制发展中国家的税收利益。如此复杂且明显不具有全面公平性的规则设计，必然会导致国际社会尤其是发展中国家的不满。OECD需要完善改革方案，处理好金额A中自动化数字服务和面向消费者业务的常规利润分割的实质性问题、面向消费者的数字企业和传统企业的利润分割一体化问题，才能推动改革共识的达成。

三 全球防止税基侵蚀方案的规则再建构

为了应对跨国企业税基侵蚀与利润转移问题，防止跨国企业利用各国的税收优惠规避征税，OECD制定了应对数字经济税收挑战的支柱二方案。针对个别国家（地区）出现征税不足的情形，支柱二方案建议授予合格国家（或地区）"征回"相应税款的权利（a Right to Tax Back），以补足至最低税水平，以确保跨国企业集团在各有关国家（或地区）的有效税率不低于经协商一致的最低水平。方案若开始全面推行，跨国企业的避税空间将被很大程度地压缩，这样就能较大程度地保障各国的税收权益。

（一）居民国与来源国的反避税规则组成

支柱二方案通过"所得纳入规则"（Income Inclusion Rule，IIR）、"转换规则"（Switch-over Rule，SOR）解

决居民国未充分征税问题。为减少企业集团内部将利润转移到实际税率低于"全球最低税率"地区的避税安排，OECD制定了所得纳入规则，即若跨国企业在境外的受控实体或分支机构在当地取得的收入适用的当地有效税率低于"全球最低税率"时，股东所在国可对此征税。该规则可以有效维护跨国公司的母公司所在国的税收利益，对企业将收入分配至低税国或者避税地的避税行为进行打击和处罚。作为配套规则，支柱二方案又引入了转换规则，即当企业在境外设立的常设机构或企业在境外不动产（非常设机构拥有的不动产）取得的利润或收益在当地适用的有效税率低于"全球最低税率"时，允许居民国将境外所得免税法转为抵免法进行税务处理，这就给居民国对此收益征税提供了依据，但同时允许抵免在境外已缴纳的税额，从而补上了目前通行的OECD《关于对所得和财产避免双重征税的税收协定范本》和联合国《关于发达国家与发展中国家间避免双重征税的协定范本》中的消除双重征税规则之间存在的漏洞。

其次，支柱二方案通过"征税不足支付规则"（Undertaxed Payments Rule，UTPR）和"应予征税规则"（Subject-to-tax Rule，STTR）解决来源国税基侵蚀问题。征税不足支付规则是指如果有关联关系的收款人取得的收入在其居民国未足额缴纳最低税额或缴纳的有效税率低于"全球最低税率"时，来源国可以对该笔款项进行源泉征税，或付款人不能就该笔款项进行税前扣除。作为对征税不足支付规则的补充，应予征税规则①要求来源国对收款人的居民国未充分征税的款项直接征收预提所得税或其他税，同时这个收入不能享受税收协定待遇。应予征税规则的应用将对总部在境外并在收入的来源国经营业务的跨国公司产生显著的影响，会削弱甚至完全抵消跨国企业在各国享受税收优惠后取得的实际好处。

上述规则设计，看似谋求法律规则的公平性，甚至对弱势来源国给予特别的关照；但是，实际上这是以法律的形式压制实质公平需求，对发展中国家尤其是弱势国家反而是不利的。

（二）发展中国家与发达国家的权利结构

支柱二方案的前提与核心在于确定"全球最低税率"，名义上将对所有国家产生正向收益。然而，静态形式规则往往无法反映动态发展的实质公平需求，如果规则被理想化和滥用，将大大限制发展中国家的发展权，新兴数字经济行业发展也将面临相似的局面，即：正当的自主性特别

---

① 根据《应对经济数字化税收挑战——支柱一和支柱二蓝图报告》的安排，应予征税规则对前述这些规则起总体补充作用，并在反避税实践中优先前述规则进行适用。

第二章 数字经济国际税收治理变革的理论创新

发展需求成为不正当的、没有规则支持和保护的行为。

支柱二方案在法律形式上保障了居民国和来源国的税基安全和公平，但前提是在经济活动正常发生的情况下，也就是说方案规则适用于经济活跃的地区和行业。如果落后地区和创新行业需要启动经济、促进增长，基于历史经验（其实也是市场经济的资本逻辑）往往急需国家乃至国际给予初期资本投入所需要的财政税收优惠支持，这就毫无疑问会出现单边、双边乃至多边的有效税率低于OECD设定的所谓"全球最低税率"的情形。一旦支柱二方案不能将这种情形排除在外，必然导致对这些国家和地区财政自主性的干涉，其本质上是对正当发展权的压制，将形成类似历史上的发达国家给发展中国家"抽梯子"的政策效应。

因此，笔者认为，支柱二方案需要特别增加反避税的排除条款，同时配套设计"视同纳税加回规则"（Deemed-tax Added-back Rule，DTABR）。即如果税收主权者单方面或者与其他主权者达成合意，给予特定地区或特定行业税收优惠，在计算"全球最低税率"时，税收优惠对应的税额应当被视同有效纳税并加总到该计算过程确定税率。这个规则不存在被跨国企业滥用进行避税的问题，因为税收优惠条件的适用仍然需要协定方确定各自的企业是不是实质性参与价值创造，是否真正符合规则设定的促进落后

053

地区和新兴行业发展的政策目标。

当然，这里还会有个疑问，那就是OECD本来是为了保障跨境交易中的国家税基的，而依照"视同纳税加回规则"的做法不但与OECD方案目标不符，而且在短期内和形式上会弱化交易各方（尤其是发展中和落后国家）的税收权益。笔者认为，一方面，这是由资本逻辑和市场悖论决定的。市场经济发展的初始启动有赖于资本的加入，但是资本追求低成本高收益，在落后地区或者新兴行业的初始投入量和风险都是巨大的，税收优惠被证明是一种有效的激励机制；进一步而言，如果没有资本推动经济的启动和发展，落后地区和新兴行业将无法产生任何税源和税基，这是成熟经济和发展中经济的现实区别，遗憾的是，发达国家往往故意忽视和掩盖这个事实。另一方面，这还涉及发展中国家的财政自主和完整性问题。如果发展中国家依据财政自主施行税收优惠措施，虽然从长远看可以得到未来税收的弥补，但当下在理论上还是在伤害自己的税基也就是公共服务能力。因此，发展中国家需要强化国家能力建设、建立完整的财政体制，利用国有资源和国有企业弥补和支撑公共服务成本。这个问题涉及更大的财政学和政治经济学问题，有待深入探讨。

由此，"视同纳税加回规则"的设定不是对国家税收主权和税基的破坏，反而是对主权的真正维护和有效培育。所以，我们需要重新评价税收优惠的正当性，尤其是重新认识OECD"BEPS行动计划"的第五项，即其长期以来坚持的所谓的"有害税收竞争"问题，以实现税收的形式公平权与经济的实质发展权之间的平衡，真正实现国际税收和世界经济的可持续发展。

结语

面对在全球数字经济发展下跨国企业跨境交易的宏微观多维框架与居民国、来源国、市场国、避税地多方格局，并且需要迫切地应对税基侵蚀、税基错配和税收脱嵌等问题，我们要拿出数字经济国际税收全球治理的中国思维与中国方案。这就需要立足中国的特色数字经济，协调技术进步、存量公平和增量共享的政策目标，通过慎重确定产业范围，科学建立税收联接度、合理设定收入门槛，同时重新认知国家角色、全面评价税收优惠和积极推动增长共享，逐步建立起数字生产和消费的耦合税制、数字与实体经济的匹配税制、税收收入与经济增长的协调税制。

第三章
数字经济国际税收治理变革的战略选择

　　基于背景梳理和理论创新,结合国际社会近年来的改革实践,在数字经济国际税收治理变革的大潮中,可以明显发现两种不同的战略路径选择。首先是经合组织提出的应对跨国公司税基侵蚀与利润转移(BEPS)的反避税战略,它具有重大的历史进步性,但同时受税收狭义化发展的影响,导致国家财政失败后的改革局限性;其次是基于"一带一路"倡议共商共建共享原则,推动建立税基共建与利润共享(New-BEPS)的国际税收合作发展战略,避免了税收狭义化和脱嵌化发展,具有树立有利于全面经济发展的改革信念的先进性。

第一节　应对税基侵蚀与利润转移(BEPS)反避税战略

　　2015年OECD出台了应对税基侵蚀与利润转移(BEPS)

行动计划的最终版本，BEPS 行动计划的提出有助于各国完善和优化其税法法律和国际税收协定，从而减少国家间的税基侵蚀与利润转移问题。

一 BEPS 反避税战略的背景与框架

从政治经济学视角来看，全球层面的以资本利润和政府税收为代表的公私利益一体互动格局的失衡，在一定程度上体现了资本与劳动的失衡。反避税战略的提出源于 20 世纪以来经济全球化的飞速发展。随着机械化的成熟和互联网技术的蓬勃发展，企业的交通运输成本和仓储成本大幅下降；除此之外，一些技术的垄断和分化使得专业化和精细化分工合作的成本更低。因此，为了实现企业利润的最大化并进一步开拓国际市场，大规模的企业往往会选择跨国的分工合作来优化生产结构。这种生产决策的结果是，跨国企业的生产环节和资金流动的分离，资本本身并不会直接带来就业和收入，而利用资本进行生产制造的过程能够创造就业机会和收入，最终导致劳动和资本的分离，而由于目前主导的分配方式更加强调资本和技术的重要性，因此会侵蚀生产环节所在国的税基，降低原有主权国家法律和税收政策的约束力。过去，由于经济和技术水平的限制，企业的经济规模小于国家的范围，因此以国家为单位的法律和政策的约束可以完全覆盖企业的经济行为，而随着经济和科技的发展，企业的经济范围扩展至全球，原有法律和政策所能够约束的税基缩小，再加上不同国家政治和战略定位的差异性，为企业提供了广大的避税空间。全球化开辟了国际避税的广大空间，企业为了实现利润最大化，充分利用各国税法和政策的差异性和优势来规避税负，而这样会损害主权国家原有的税收收入，影响市场经济的公平运行，导致国际税收法律的失衡。由于全球化的商业形式变化，以及国际金融危机的影响，多个国家财政出现了不同程度的赤字，为了缓解财政危机，多国开始展开打击严重的跨国避税行为，BEPS反避税战略应运而生。

BEPS反避税战略的议题共15项，涉及国际税收问题的方方面面，但出发点都是围绕反避税展开，可以说，BEPS反避税战略是国际社会为反避税而形成的初步共识，在国际税收领域具有跨时代的意义，从双重征税的问题向双重不征税的问题的转变，BEPS行动计划所提出的应对数字经济的挑战等在当时具有前瞻性的观点也引领了近年来国际反避税浪潮的趋势。从内容上来看，BEPS反避税战略在反避税的结构上相对完整，有助于帮助各国完善国际税收规则，减少国家之间的制度冲突和缺口，减少避税的漏洞；从实践上来看，多国反避税的战略共识有助于各国实现自上而下的税收征管合作，增大信息的透明度和征管的效率，进而有利于打击跨国公司的国家避税，减少国家的财政流失。除此之外，从BEPS反避税战略的制定和完善的机制来看，BEPS反避税战略尽管是在G20的领导下建立，但它让发展中国家也能够平等地参与战略的研究，并充分发表自己的意见和看法，有助于发展中国家在参与国际税收制度制定的过程中提高在国际税收领域的政治地位，充分体现了BEPS反避税战略的开放性和包容性。

二 BEPS反避税战略的本质与问题

（一）国家财政定位的畸形影响反避税战略的实施

BEPS反避税战略的有效实施，不仅要具备科学可行的实施方案，还要求各国具有强烈的反避税意愿，有相对一致的财政定位。从国家征税的动机来看，反避税难度大的根源并不是国家之间的税收竞争，而是不同国家税收立场的差异。假设每个国家都以税收作为财政收入的主要来源，建立完备无偏的税收制度，那对于企业来说，整体税负不变，只改变了纳税的地点，因此不存在强烈的国际避税动机；而如果一些国家不以税收作为财政支柱，而是强调税收的政策刺激作用，那么就会形成税收洼地，造成税基的流失。

　　20世纪供给学派的观点强调经济的自由主义，认为需求的刺激能够对市场经济造成积极影响。在供给学派的影响下，美国在20世纪80年代开始实施大规模的减税刺激政策。尽管减税政策在短期内刺激了经济增长、创造了就业，但也导致了财政赤字，增大了美国的财政负担。再加上之后金融危机的影响，进一步打击了美国财政的收入。可见，从长期来看，仅强调税收的政策导向和市场效率是不可持续的，税收的狭义化发展将导致国家财政失败，并由此带来进步性改革的局限性。现代国家本质上应该是税收国家，税收应该作为更加持续和稳定的财政工具来保障国家经济共同体的正常运转。税收作为公共财政支出的重要来源，在长期应实现以支定收的可持续发展路线，进而保障政府的功能，满足经济社会发展的需要；而如果国家的财政更多地依赖于债务收入，政府的功能便会在一定程度上被削弱，无法满足社会经济发展的需要。从税收的原则来看，税收制度不仅仅是为了实现市场经济的良性发展，保障纳税人的财产以及维持基本的市场运行秩序等税收中性的要求，还要实现对纳税人财富的初次分配的公平调节，减少市场经济的缺陷，以此来促进社会的公平和经济的良性发展。为了发挥中央财政的宏观调节作用，完善税收国家的税收制度体系，中国在1994年进行了分税制改革，着重突出了税收在财政收入中的关键地位，并增大了财政收入在 GDP 中的占比。1994 年，财政收入占 GDP 的比重仅为 11%，而 2019 年该比重则增长到了 28.14%。中国财政收入占比的增加，有助于国家发挥宏观调节作用，满足公共服务的需要。从横向比较来看，中国的财政收入占比没有高于一般国际水平，在 2019 年中国的财政收入占比比美国的 32.66% 约低了 4.5 个百分点，在社会保障和福利等方面仍存在发展的空间。

（二）BEPS 行动计划仍未触及反避税的根本缺陷

BEPS 行动计划的内容加强了国家层面税收法律的规范性，例如提供了一些反避税的基本制度框架，包括转让定价的调整，受控外国公司的规定等，这有利于帮助一些国际税收制度发展较晚的国家建立基本的国际反避税制度，我国特别纳税调整的相关法律法规也在此基础上进行了规范和完善。除此之外，BEPS 行动计划强调明确国际税收征管的方式，加强国际征管的合作，从而提高国际税收征管的效率，降低信息不对称和权力受限等反避税阻力。由于国际税收的范围超过了国家的界限，因此只有当各国的反避税制度能够实现一定程度的统一后，才能够有效进行国际层面的反避税，可以说制度的共识和一致是反避税制度实施的重要前提。

但 BEPS 行动计划需要的专业性和技术性较强。例如，为了解决转让定价问题，BEPS 行动计划提出了多种方案来实现企业利润分配的合理性，但是在国际反避税的实际征管环节，税务机关往往优先考虑转让定价调整方式的便捷性和可操作性，因此技术性高操作性低的转让定价调整方式即使效果更好，也仍得不到广泛的应用。这从一个角度说明，反避税战略的选择要强调其效率，避免纸上谈兵。

由于 OECD 本身组织性质的限制，OECD 并不能建立超越国家主权的单一征税的国际层面的税收制度。而 21 世纪以来，欧美国家（地区）的经济方式出现了不同层次的分化，欧洲一些老牌发达国家依然依赖生产制造业进行发展，而美国则率先开启了互联网经济的发展，并在电商和社交等多个方向处于相对垄断的地位。由于各国经济的生产结构和要素构成以及资金流动的模式都有所差异，因此各国面临的反避税问题也有所不同，不同国家的不同反避税诉求影响了最终统一性制度的形成和落实。除此之外，排除经济模式的差异因素，发达国家的整体反避税诉求是建立在资本控制和利益至上基础上的，并没有考虑国际税收秩序本身的可持续性和公平性，因此并不能解决长期的问题。此外，狭义的国际税收只是主权国家税收的一个分支部分，因此仅从国际税收的维度来改革反避税战略，并不能触及问题的本质。

（三）数字经济商业模式下新的避税缺口需要更深层次的改革

尽管在 BEPS 行动计划中第一项行动计划就是对数字经济的应对，但是由于其改革的维度仍只停留在反避税层面，并没有触及利润分配的方式和处理的原则，因此并不能从根源上解决数字经济下的国际税收问题。在数字经济的发展下，数字作为一个新的生产要素，在产品价值链中发挥着愈加重要的作用，这一生产要素的投入通过互联网信息技术实现，不受地理的限制，数字价值的实现表现为一种多元主体协同共创的模式，具体来说数字价值的实现过程不仅需要企业的平台技术支持，公众和用户的参与和贡献也是必不可少的一部分，而这些价值的实现较少地依托于物理实体的存在，即使不在收入来源国设立常设机构也不影响数字价值的产生，在这样的经济模式下，继续采用常设机构作为营业利润税权划分的门槛，会增大跨国企业的避税空间，对现行的税收制度造成扭曲：一方面跨国企业会通过无形资产的转让定价来规避在居民国的纳税，另一方面跨国企业可以通过减少常设机构的设立来规避在市场国的纳税。综上考虑，不论是数字经济输入国还是数字经济的输出国，其税基在现行的税收制度下都可能会遭到侵蚀。因此从长期来看，需要建立新的经济关联原则和税收分配原则，达成全球性的国际税收共识，只有在这样的前提下，数字经济带来的避税问题才能够得到根本性的解决。

第二节 推动税基共建与利润共享（New-BEPS）合作发展战略

面对全球反避税战略的发展困境，中国需要坚持供给侧结构性改革，加强系统性和针对性，基于反避税的困境进行更深层次的改革。从国家税收的角度来看，应重视国家主权的建设和国际地位的提升，积极引导世界的多极化；从整体的发展战略来看，中国应坚持中国特色社会主义道路，充分发挥中国特色社会主义优势，以合作共赢方式推进"一带一路"倡议下的人类命运共同体建设。

一 "一带一路"新发展格局与数字经济发展新需求

（一）"一带一路"的互联互通与"双循环"发展的新格局

1."一带一路"的互联互通

2013 年，中国首次正式提出"一带一路"倡议，构建"丝绸之路经济带"和"21 世纪海上丝绸之路"，与共建国家在经济、政治、文化等领域开展全方位、深层次的合作，形成紧密的伙伴关系，打造"共商、共建、共享"的人类命运共同体。"友好合作，互利共赢"一直是我国在对外交往中秉持的核心理念，在新时代背景下，"一带一路"倡议是我国对外开放的重要实践，是实现政治互信、经济相容的重要平台。政治沟通、设施联通、贸易畅通、资金融通、民心相通的"五通"政策不仅有利于拓展我国"走出去"的广度和深度，而且顺应了相关各国高质量快速发展的需求以及经济全球化的时代要求，提供了一个在合作中共同发展的包容性平台。

习近平新时代中国特色社会主义建设提出了创新、协调、绿色、开放、共享的新发展理念，该五大发展理念的基点是共同利益和整体利益，在相互贯通和相互促进中实现个体与整体的共赢。"一带一路"倡议的深入推进正是该五大发展理念在我国对外交往中的深刻体现，有利于拉动共建国家的经济增长，改善当地人民的生活质量；有利于形成富有活力、开放共赢、公正合理、平衡普惠的经济模式，促进区域经济一体化；有利于推动全球治理体系的变革，带领世界经济走上强劲、可持续、平衡、包容的发展之路；有利于构建休戚与共的人类命运共同体。

至2018年，中国与共建"一带一路"国家（地区）的进出口总额达6500亿美元。至2021年，共建"一带一路"

国家（地区）已增至140个国家和30个国际组织，中国共计签署200份文件。2019年1月至7月，中国"走出去"企业对52个共建"一带一路"国家（地区）的新增投资总额达79.7亿美元，并购共计36起，亚投行成员国达63国。随着中国与共建"一带一路"国家（地区）的经贸往来广泛深入，各方之间的合作交流早已超越了经济领域，启动了大批务实合作、造福民众的项目，构建起全方位、复合型的互联互通伙伴关系，开创了共同发展的新前景。

2. "双循环"发展的新格局

新冠肺炎疫情对世界政治经济格局造成了巨大的冲击，给全球治理带来了新的挑战。中国与共建"一带一路"国家（地区）守望相助，在合作中共克时艰，继续共同推进"一带一路"建设，互相提供防疫物资及技术上的援助，维持各方的经济社会平稳发展，向国际社会传递了信心和力量，为全球抗疫合作和经济复苏做出了重要贡献。为应对疫情常态化防控下新的国内外发展形势，中国着手打造"以国内大循环为主体、国内国际双循环相互促进的新发展格局"。新冠肺炎疫情期间，受益于"一带一路"倡议的"五通"政策，中国的对外贸易在2020年1月至9月实现了0.7%的正增长，因此打造"双循环"新发展格局时，与"一带一路"建设的对接直接影响中国整体经济发展质量以及对外开放的战略定位。"中蒙俄"、

"新亚欧大陆桥"、"中国－中亚－西亚"、"中国－中南半岛"、"中巴"以及"孟中印缅"六大经济走廊的建设是"一带一路"建设的核心,不仅贯穿多国,有利于全方位实现互联互通,而且涉及中国多个省份,因此结合"一带一路"建设的六大经济走廊构建"双循环"体系,对拉动中国内需和促进对外合作均具有重大的战略意义。

"双循环"的构建与"一带一路"建设的对接具有现实可行性。自"一带一路"倡议提出以来,中国不断与相关国家开展投融资合作,给予大力的资金支持,相关国家(地区)获得的中国的对外直接投资存量逐年增加,说明中国与其资金融通水平较高且稳定;中国与共建"一带一路"国家(地区)在农产品和工业产品贸易方面已经构建了"外循环",因此具备产业合作基础;六大经济走廊的基础设施建设逐步完善,为"双循环"的构建提供了硬件条件;中国数字经济飞速发展,与共建"一带一路"国家(地区)在新兴领域的交流合作进一步加深,有利于推进"数字丝绸之路"的建设,实现数字经济与实体经济的融合,进而更好地服务于"双循环"的构建。

(二)数字经济与"一带一路"发展的新需求

1. 数字经济对全球治理的影响

随着人工智能、大数据、云计算等数字技术的飞速发展和广泛应用,数字经济成为经济效能提升的重要引擎,各国纷纷出台数字经济相关的计划、战略或议程,试图抓住这一发展机遇。数字经济时代下,不仅生产生活方式发生了巨大变化,而且全球治理模式处在瓦解、重构、变革、创新的重要阶段。数字经济虽然为促进贸易便利化等方面带来了好处,但在维护网络安全、分配跨国权益等方面为全球治理带来挑战和困境,这也反映出数字经济时代对全球治理产生了完全不同于传统经济时代的重大影响,对构建一个公平、开放、包容、共赢的全球治理新体系提出了迫切要求。

从数字技术、数字贸易、数字金融、数字政务以及数字安全五个不同的角度进行分析,可以发现数字经济对全球治理同时产生了正面和负面影响。第一,从数字技术的角度看,数字经济有利于利用线上沟通技术为国家之间的谈判磋商创造更加便利的条件,有利于为世界经济中新型业态的出现和发展提供技术支撑,有利于开展数据分析以实现科学合理的全球治理。但是,相应的负面影响包括:种类繁多的数字技术会增加国际认证标准统一的难度;不同国家和地区之间的数字经济发展水平差异较大,数字技术的广泛应用会进一步拉大数字鸿沟;数字技术因其特有的虚拟性,极易降低作恶成本,一旦被不正当使用会激化地区间矛盾,甚至破坏国家间的稳定关系。第二,从数字贸易的角度看，数字经济使得贸易具有普惠性，有利于依靠数字平台提高世界整体的贸易福利，有利于将生产者、消费者和政府在一个平台上联系起来形成贸易生态，降低贸易壁垒，更有效地解决跨国贸易中产生的争端。但是，相应的负面影响包括：数据安全及隐私保护成为亟待解决的问题；平台型市场结构极易形成新型垄断，随之而来的资源重组和权力重构对政府与市场的关系、消费者与企业的关系产生了巨大的冲击，如何应对这种新型垄断以及明确价值创造和利润分配的标准是数字经济时代下全球治理的重中之重。第三，从数字金融的角度看，有利于优化全球资本要素的配置，促进全球金融业的数字化升级，有利于为所有群体提供无差别的金融服务，在全球范围内消除绝对贫困。但是，相应的负面影响包括：各国对数据安全的认定标准不一，不利于维护跨国权益；数字金融诈骗更加隐蔽，增加系统性金融风险。第四，从数字政务角度看，有利于提高双边或多边政治经济合作的效率，实现协同治理；有利于促进数据共享，实现智慧治理。但是，相应的负面影响包括：为各国政府对识别数据信息和安全防护增加了难度。第五，从数字安全的角度看，有利于共同建设、维护和治理网络安全空间；有利于根据国际组织、政府、企业和个人等不同的主体，提高相对应的信息防护等级。但是，相应的负面影响包括虚拟货币、区块链技术等数字技术的使用本身就存在数据安全问题。

2. "一带一路"共建中的数字经济合作

相较于传统经济时代，数字经济时代下的全球治理模式存在诸多不同，不仅受到政治、经济、文化和国际话语权等传统因素的影响，而且受到数字经济本身带来的冲击。值得注意的是，数字经济打破了长久以来发达国家主导的利益保守性的全球经济体系及治理模式，正在重构全新的世界经济发展格局。在数字经济时代，发展中国家和新兴经济体发展迅猛，在新格局中的地位和话语权不断提升，全球治理体系也应朝着更加公平、合理、包容、平衡的方向演进。在此背景下，中国提出以"共商、共建、共享"为原则的"一带一路"倡议，体现出中国在构建全球治理新格局中的大国担当，有利于保障各方在合作中共享发展成果。

传统经济时代下的全球治理模式由发达国家主导，其鲜明的特点是中心化、纵向、单一，具有很强的利益保守性，发展中国家和新兴经济体完全被排除在分享既得利益的范围之外。其结果不仅有失公平，而且导致全球治理目标的分配只能从全球层面传递至区域层面，再一步步最终分解至国家和国内层面，最终破坏了全球治理的一致性和整体性。在数字经济时代，数字化贸易带来的价值创造和利润分配成为区域一体化的动力，相应的全球治理也应形成横向、多样化的模式。中国积极参与构建数字经济时代下全球治理新格局的理念始终是推动多边主义区域一体化,"一带一路"倡议的深入推进正是该理念的深刻实践。我国利用国内数字经济飞速发展的优势,正在打造"数字丝绸之路",目前与共建"一带一路"国家在数字经济领域已开展了一定数量的合作。例如,2019年中国与东盟十国签署了《东盟互联互通总体规划2025》和《中国-东盟智慧城市合作倡议领导人声明》,为未来双方在数字经济领域的互联互通做出了展望。

我国在应对数字经济时代时应做到如下三点。第一,坚定打造"人类命运共同体"的信念,在追求自身利益时兼顾别国利益,推动"数字丝绸之路"建设,真正做到互联互通和共商共建共享。第二,求同存异,采用协商的方式解决争端,实现协同治理和多边治理,推动多边主义区域一体化。第三,进一步增强我国的数字经济实力,提升国际地位和话语权,为共建"一带一路"的发展中国家和新兴经济体发声,构建公平、包容的全球治理模式。

二 数字经济时代"一带一路"国际税收治理的中国思路

国际税收治理是全球治理体系的重要组成部分。中国与共建"一带一路"国家(地区)开展广泛而深入的经贸往来，加强国家间的税务合作、优化税收环境、提高税收确定性始终是"一带一路"倡议关注的重点。尤其是面对数字经济的冲击，传统的税收规则不再适用，价值创造和利润分配的认定直接影响一国的国际话语权。因此，数字经济时代下国际税收关系需要共建"一带一路"国家（地区）共同治理。所以，我国作为倡议国，可以在国际税收治理改革方面提出税基共建与利润共享（New-BEPS）的合作发展战略。

新时代的国际税收治理因不同经济体的道路选择而呈现迥异特色。为应对数字经济的冲击，OECD提出税基侵蚀与利润转移（BEPS）行动计划，该计划强调分好蛋糕，在存量竞争中寻求公平；而"一带一路"建设则旨在集中资源做大蛋糕，在合作中寻求增量共享。税基共建与利润共享为建立与"一带一路"建设配套的国际税收规则，实现"一带一路"共商、共建、共享原则在国际税收领域的具体化，提供了一种思路和方案。

（一）BEPS行动计划：国际税收应对战略的进步性与局限性

国际金融危机之后，为了重构国际税收和经济秩序，应对政府收支失衡，以经济合作与发展组织（OECD）为主导的BEPS行动计划应运而生，该行动计划旨在建立一个在全球范围内公平和现代化的国际税收体系，其基本框架包括正在推行的应对税基侵蚀与利润转移合作、情报交换和协定多边工具等。这些对提高税收确定性、保障财政安全具有积极的进步意义。例如，在国际转让定价领域，BEPS行动计划依据"转让定价结果与价值创造相一致"理念提出的价值创造论具有重大的历史进步性，以《转让定价文档与国别报告指南》强化全球征管合作，达成税法规范的统一性和一致性，对于全球税收秩序在形式正义和程序合理层面具有重大意义。

然而，BEPS行动计划继续坚持"独立交易原则"，仅仅让步承认交易利润分割法并仍然着重强调资本（无形资产）的剩余利润分配权，又不无遗憾地显示出一定局限性。一个典型的案例是，2016年8月，欧盟委员会裁定爱尔兰政府与苹果公司的预约定价安排违反了欧盟的禁止"政府补贴"法律，属于"非法国家援助"，要求爱尔兰政府向苹果公司补征130亿欧元税款，招致美国对德意志银行施加140亿美元罚款的非对称性报复措施。此等纷纭复杂的案例说明，BEPS行动计划形成的统一的转让定价报告制度、自动情报交换安排和修订税收协定的多边工具等规则体系初具现代国际税收秩序的形式特征。然而，在非独立不等价与独立不等价的交换普遍存在的情况下，BEPS行动计划拘泥于存量的竞争和分配，构造的是一种以反避税为主的，扎起篱笆"闭门争税"的相对消极的秩序。

由此可见，虽然 BEPS 行动计划为共同应对国际税收挑战提供了良好范式，但仍存在固守新自由主义思维的弊端。BEPS 行动计划主要是危机应对机制，将主要精力集中于打击避税地，且仍未摆脱固化中心国家地位的惯性思维，无法从根本上对不平等的国际税收利益分配格局进行调整。尤其是，BEPS 行动计划对于帮助发展中国家和低收入国家夯实财政治理基石这一完善全球经济治理关键手段的重视程度不够，不能在根本上助力全球经济走向均衡发展的道路。

（二）New-BEPS：国际税收应对战略的升级版与预建构

中国与共建"一带一路"国家（地区）分享优质产能，共商项目投资、共建基础设施、共享合作成果，真正实现"五通"，并最终共同打造政治互信、经济相容、文化包容的利益共同体、命运共同体和责任共同体。因此，应当认识到，"一带一路"不只意味着企业"走出去"，更是一种区域和全球资源配置新模式，即世界经济和社会的全球化新模式。

如果说 BEPS 行动计划强调分好蛋糕，意在存量竞争中寻求一种形式公平,"一带一路"则旨在集中资源做大蛋糕,在合作中寻求增量共享。由此,税基共建与利润共享的国际税收治理新战略呼之欲出。New-BEPS 是"一带一路"共商、共建、共享原则在国际税收领域的具体应用,应发展成为 BEPS 行动计划的中国优化升级版。在"一带一路"包容性增长理念推动下,New-BEPS 打造的是一种更具主动性的"走出去"、增长型和共享型秩序,其有赖于市场增强型有为政府的积极财政政策的推行,是在区域间建立以公平利润原则、公式分配法、地域特殊性优势分配权、行业税收"安全港"规则和区域税务特区制度等为内容的国际税收创新体系,并将以简单、确定、高效和公平的国际税制推动税基共建与利润共享、经济发展和实质性社会公平正义秩序的实现。

综上,全球化困局将催生国际税收秩序现代化的深刻变革,包括发达国家提出的以有限干预、消极权利和形式正义为主要特征的 BEPS 行动计划,也应该包括以中国为代表的发展中国家和新兴经济体提出的以积极秩序和实质正义为特征的 New-BEPS 改革方案。递进式、体系性的国际税收秩序重构将进一步表明:税收不应只是竞争的标的,而更应成为合作的推进剂。全球化不应当也不会停滞,而是将以一种崭新的更健康的秩序展开。

第四章
数字经济国际税收治理变革的政策设计

数字经济国际税收治理变革的理论创新与战略选择，最终需要落脚到具体的政策设计。观察近年来数字经济国际税改实践，主要形成了基于典型国家的单边主义措施和经合组织多边合作框架的"双支柱"改革方案。国际社会改革方案的博弈，催促中国明晰自身的利益关切，表明国家政策立场，并前瞻性地设计好应对策略。

第一节 数字经济国际税收治理变革的国际博弈

综观近年来如火如荼的数字经济国际税收改革方案的全球博弈，首先表现为一些国家提出的数字服务税的单边主义措施，尽管其具有很大的历史正当性，但仍需反思其规则的可行性和治理的争议性；其次是经合组织提出的基于多边合作框架的双支柱改革方案，作为全球焦点，其在确立市场国公平税收权益的同时限制了新兴行业/落后地区的财政自主权和发展公平权，这一改革兼具进步性与保守性，需要进行利益再平衡和规则再建构。

一 数字服务税的单边主义措施

百年变局大背景下，数字经济的发展为国际税收的改革带来了前所未有的挑战。数字经济的高度流动性、依赖无形资产等特点加剧了世界经济供需失衡，而传统的国际税收规则无法提供科学有效的办法分割税基，甚至连最基本的征税权问题都无法解决。在这一背景下，生产国与市场国的税收经济矛盾日益突出，英国、印度等部分国家为了保护自己的经济利益，通过开征数字服务税抢先采取了单边行动，掀起了争夺市场国征税权的热潮。

（一）数字服务税的出台与各方观点

1. 各国数字服务税[①]开征

关于数字服务税，又称数字税，有狭义和广义的概念。狭义上是指对提供数字服务的平台（主要大型互联网企业）根据其数字业务的收入所征收的一种税，广义上是

---

① 数字服务税是数字经济国际税收改革中对于基于数字经济的新设税制的统称，主要表现为一些国家开征的大同小异的数字服务税。

指对各种涉及数字服务的交易所征收的税收。起初，数字服务税是欧盟应对数字经济采取的一种临时性措施，实施的原因是：数字企业以较低的成本在全球内从事跨境交易，通过向用户提供数字服务及产品获取高额利润，但是这部分收入并未在相关的市场国征收任何的税负，造成数字企业与其他传统企业的严重税负不公平，因此采取单边措施来弥补数字企业与市场国辖区内其他企业的税负差距。目前对于数字服务税的性质尚无统一的定论，最早是由法国、英国以及西班牙率先采取的单边措施，随后有印度、巴西、肯尼亚等十多个国家相继在近两年计划开征，但考虑到国内外经济走势，也有一些国家如波兰选择中途停止征收数字服务税。由于各国数字服务税制度的具体实践，在课征范围、起征点以及税率方面有较大的差异，因此实施起来也存在一定的难度与困境。

2. 关于数字服务税的争议

目前数字服务税的反对方提出的主要理由包括：会导致双重征税或过度征税，而且会使达成全球一致解决方案更加困难；这种做法对大型数字企业是一种税收歧视，会使数字经济企业发展产生扭曲；数字服务税会影响税收公平，是一种不合理的应对措施；数字服务税不包括在税收协定的协调范围之内；等等。具体分析如下。

一是数字服务税的经济后果构成不公平的税收歧视。

法国作为欧盟第一个开征数字服务税的国家，其举措引起了美国的不满，2019年7月美国对法国开征数字服务税展开了301调查。主要围绕税收歧视、税收公平性、不合理性三个方面展开。首先，由于美国企业大部分满足7.5亿欧元的收入门槛，美国认为法国这一做法明显是针对美国企业的一种歧视待遇。其次，法国数字服务税追溯至2019年1月1日，这样会增加纳税人的计税难度，影响税收的公平性。此外，美国认为数字服务税这一举措有悖国际税收的规范性。还有一些观点认为，数字企业会将数字服务税新增的税负转嫁给其他企业和消费者，对于未能转嫁出去的税负可能会造成数字企业机会成本的增加，从而降低投资回报率，影响企业盈利能力和盈利水平。

二是数字服务税的计税依据依然存在价值创造问题。目前对于推行数字服务税较大的困难在于难以确定计税依据，可以看出现行措施中主要以收入、流量和用户作为征税对象。第一，以收入为计税依据，该方案主要是欧盟提出的"双门槛"方案，以大多数跨国公司每年全球营业收入在7.5亿欧元以上为依据。有一些反对的声音认为，对收入进行征税而非净所得，这样对利润较少或者亏损的企业而言是不公平的。第二，以流量为计税依据，主要是以比特币为代表，将数据看作一种流量，但是数据的确权具有不确定性，并且缺乏合理的定价机制。数字服务税也是随着数字经济的发展而产生的一种被动性措施。由于随着网络自身的发展，链接的成本趋于零，关于数据的确权和利益分配问题目前无法给出真正完善的答案，所以这种以流量为计税依据的科学性还有待考证。第三，以用户价值创造为计税依据，目前实行数字服务税的国家，均突出用户在价值创造中发挥的作用，所以征税权归属于用户所处的国家。但是，对于用户通过参与的形式是否为交易创造了价值，以及怎样产生价值，创造价值的规模是多少，目前尚无统一的标准。当市场国一方强调数据本身具有价值的时候，也有观点认为数据本身不具有价值，它仅仅是一种原始的加工材料。如果按照用户的价值贡献确定计税依据，那么对于数据产生的是积极的还是消极的影响无法准确地划分。

三是法律层面税收协定协调存在争议。数字服务税在立法方面还存在较多的难题，例如，数字服务税是否能够适用于税收协定还存在争议，主要焦点在于居民国没有理由为企业在市场国缴纳的数字服务税提供税收抵免，因此可能会造成各界所担心的双重征税的问题。根据传统的税收协定的规定，只有当缔约国一方的居民企业在另一方缔约国境内作为常设机构时，其在另一方缔约国取得的营业利润才应该归属于该国，否则只应当在其居民国缴纳税款。然而由于数字经济无形性的特点，跨国数字企业在另一方缔约国无须构成常设机构便可以获取利润。这不符合之前税收协定的规定，因此无法对数字企业征税，如果将数字服务税归属于税收协定范围的税种，则会出现违背税收协定初衷的情形。这种冲突的存在便导致了数字服务税定性问题的争论。欧盟认为数字服务税是一种间接税，从而避开了税收协定的适用条款。反对者认为虽然数字服务税没有类似所得税对净利润征税，但适用远远低于所得税的税率，这说明已经考虑了成本费用的扣除，因此按照税收协定范本中第二条第四款的规定，数字服务税属于所得税性质的税收，应当纳入税收协定的调整范畴。

3. 数字服务税的可行性

一是确认数字服务税的性质为新的租金类型。目前对于数字服务税是直接税还是间接税的定性问题尚未明确，明确数字服务税的性质，并给定一个合理的解释或许是最好的理论依据。可以将数字服务税看作一种针对地域性特殊平台的租金税，这样可以解决数字经济下产生的新问题。[1]将数字服务税视为租金包括两个理想的特性。一方面，这种性质的税收收入对于经济的扭曲程度最小。另一方面，如果可以判定租金的专属地点，就可以进一步解决

---

[1] Cui W. The Digital Services Tax on the Verge of Implementation[J]. Canadian Tax Journal, 2019, 67(4).

划分征税权的问题，使税收管辖权归属于租金所在的税收管辖区，从而避免重复征税的风险。此外，租金的地点确定可以运用已有的税收原理、框架进行解析。

对于大型跨国企业征收数字服务税实际上是一种价值消耗的补偿，因此在一定程度上，跨国企业占用了该国的平台，消费者作为价值创造的新主体，赋予了数字资源大部分的价值。将数字服务税看作一种租金可能产生目的地、来源地或者居住地等税收管辖区，因此"用户价值创造"地不能仅仅局限于消费者所在地。[①] 在这种视角下，对于数字服务税支持的理由在于它允许将数字平台赚取的租金视为由产生这种租金的国家所得，然而在传统的国际税收中，由于拘泥于常设机构的认定问题，来源国获得这部分租金的权利是不被认可的。然而针对平台租金征税应该作为制定数字服务税的主要动机，因此租金性质的数字服务税也可以作为助推多边谈判的关键因素。

二是在关联度概念上打通生产者和消费者剩余。英国最早提出来用户价值创造的概念，欧盟进一步阐释了相关提法，认为相关国家可以因其用户对价值创造具有重要贡

---

① Cui W. The Digital Services Tax: A Conceptual Defense[J]. Tax L. Rev., 2019.

第四章 数字经济国际税收治理变革的政策设计

献而对提供特定数字服务的企业课税,并以企业提供这些数字服务的收入而非净所得为应纳税所得额,[1]正是由于用户的参与为数字经济带来了价值从而构成了征税的基础。实际上,"市场国"概念的出现以及带来的新的征税权问题催生了数字服务税改革,因此需要为其赋予征税的正确依据以及基本原则。关联度问题应该作为国际税收的起点,这事实上确定了征税权的正当性,并且明确了征税对象、主体、标准与范围。[2]关联度其实就是价值创造地原则的原型。由于数字经济的特殊性决定了可以在无实体的条件下实现经营,交换过程中没有直接对价以及无形资产实现更广泛的运用等,直接给以传统的常设机构为征税依据的国际税收规则带来了巨大的挑战,那么为什么可以将征税权赋予市场国呢?有什么理论依据?

主要推动因素在于打通生产者与消费者的概念,建立在"供需利润观"的基础上,打造税收共同体理念。首先,生产者和消费者的交易过程,实际上是两个生产者之间进行的实用价值交换过程。所谓的消费者概念其实已经发生了转换,这里的消费者已经成为具有创造价值能力的

---

[1] 张智勇.数字服务税:正当的课税抑或服务贸易的壁垒?[J].国际税收,2020(04).
[2] 曹明星.OECD数字税改方案述评:理论阐释、权益衡平与规则建构.[J].税务研究,2021(06).

生产者。交易过程实际上是生产者与生产者进行交换的过程，如果我们承认国家征税是基于政府贡献而进行的成本补偿和收益分享，[①]那么显然生产者 A 和生产者 B 将因为提供不同的使用价值进行交易形成交换价值，而分别就其生产使用价值的成本和交换价值中的利润，对各自的国家承担消费税和所得税的纳税义务，就解决了生产者 B 也就是消费者所在市场国征税权的依据问题。

（二）数字服务税中的对抗与博弈

目前来看，达成统一合作是一个漫长过程。从以往的经验看，强国更倾向于采用单边措施，弱国更倾向于合作，然而数字服务税恰恰造成了相反的局面，英法等数字经济相对较弱的国家率先开展了单边税收措施，而美国却主张进行合作，其背后有着复杂的原因。

1. 国家政府与私人企业的不平衡性

税收是企业与政府唯一联系较为紧密的渠道，同时也是长期以来双方博弈的焦点，跨国公司在不断扩充自己实力的同时，也提高了规避税收的能力。但是当国家面对联合起来的数字企业巨头时，双方的实力形成了极强的不平

[①] 曹明星，杜建伟.私人交换＋公私交换：从政府贡献视角补全可比交易全景.税务研究 [J]. 2020（7）.

衡性，政府同样面临着巨大挑战，因此在这种情形下，各国政府联合起来相互合作不失为一个最佳的选择，这种来自政府与私人企业的力量不平衡性逐渐成为推动国际合作的内生动力。英法等国家相较于美国更先而且更深层次地经历了这种不平衡性对抗，它们受到的冲击更强，理论上来讲应该更倾向于合作，然而这些国家率先采取了单边措施，一个很大的原因是财政体系的不健全以及国家财政主格的失衡问题，这是存在于发达国家根深蒂固的问题。英、法、美等国面对数字经济的冲击应该都有要进行合作的意愿，但是它们的意愿程度存在较大的差异，因此迟迟不能达成统一意向。

2. 市场主体的空间不对称性

一些国家作为主要的市场国率先采取单边行动。从数字服务税适用的格局来看，可以主要划分为三个板块。第一板块是美国和中国，美国有大量数字企业，而且涉及跨国业务较多，中国的数字企业主要在国内经营，较少涉及数字服务税问题，这类国家不适用于单边数字服务税。第二板块是以欧洲国家为主的市场国。第三板块是以印度为代表的一些技术相对落后的数字经济消费国。征收数字服务税实际上真正有利于处于后两个板块的国家。数字经济下产生了"市场国"，造成了市场主体的消费具有很强的单一性，技术输出国和市场国之间也存在很大的不可逆转的特点，因此在一定程度上限制了后续的调整与发展，因此数字服务税只能片面地满足一方的利益，如果要达成各方满意的状态，推进合作是十分必要的举措。

（三）数字服务税的未来出路

1. 数字服务税可以作为一种补充措施

目前学术界和税务界专家对数字服务税负面和批判的声音比较多，《数字服务税提案》被贴上是一种下下策、经济上权宜之计的标签，一些反对者甚至坚持认为采取双边措施是唯一的解决途径。因此应该更加理性辩证地看待数字服务税的适用情况。例如，将数字服务税看作租金，实际上从根本上确定了国家之间技术的强弱对比，即使是知识产权技术主要归属于美国，通过数字平台分布在全球其他地方的技术所赚取的租金可以视为在该国产生的，这种解释极大程度上可以改变对数字服务税的偏见，事实上也可以促使各国产生新的国际合作与对税基重新划分的共识。

2. 理想状态的合作达成

数字服务税的发展过程最初从 2015 年 BEPS 包容性框架下的第一项行动计划"应对数字经济的税收挑战"——主要围绕数字服务税的讨论展开，再到后面发布的双支柱方案，支柱一确定了市场国的征税权问题，不过是一种利益集团内部的手段，支柱二确定了全球最低税率，旨在解决全球反税基侵蚀问题，实际上也存在公平的陷阱问题。国际税收的问题自始至终不仅仅是各个国家经济、技术的对抗，其背后还有国家实力强弱的对比，要实现数字服务税全球治理的共识，不应该仅仅局限于应对方案的提出，更应该站在人类命运共同体的角度，考虑各个国家长期以来存在的税收制度理念的差异，以及数字服务税改革会对某些国家造成的潜在损失。由于没有一个超国家权力的实体存在，一直以来是以OECD作为数字服务税税收治理的主要政策讨论平台，在方案推进的过程中，不应该仅仅局限于某一个集团或者大国的利益，更要考虑技术弱国和欠发达地区的利益，只有以全局思维和公平视角出发去解决问题，才有可能带来更多国家可以接受的结果。因此，应对数字服务税的全球治理问题，只有平衡好各个经济体利益方之间由变革带来的成本和收益问题，才有可能真正推动国际共识的达成。

二　双支柱方案的多边合作框架

单边措施必然导致国际税收纷争不断，尽管联合国提出了基于双边税收协定谈判的改良方案，但是无休无止的讨价还价，除了在过程上有助于在争论博弈中推动最终共识的达成外，目前在实际层面仍然有赖于更多方面的集中智慧、利益协调，在一种包容性框架下尽早达成全球性改革方案。由此，基于G20背书的OECD的多边主义数字税改方案，就成为当前大家寄望甚深的途径。经过多轮博弈，OECD最后出台的双支柱方案仍然充满争议，达成全球共识依然困难重重，需要更多的经济妥协和更大的政治决断。

（一）双支柱方案的国际背景与政策应对

1. 方案的背景框架

从2013年起，OECD就提出了BEPS行动计划并致力于构建一个包容性框架，2020年新冠肺炎疫情的蔓延也对世界各国提出了新的要求，即在尽量短的时间内形成受国际社会一致认可的改革解决方案、共同应对数字经济国际税收治理面临的挑战。2020年10月12日，OECD发布《应对经济数字化税收挑战——支柱一和支柱二蓝图报告》，为国际税收体系的改革提供了更具体的方案。2020年11月的G20会议也将"继续推动双支柱方案，建立一个公平、可持续的现代化国际税收体系"作为一大议题。

支柱一也被称为"修订的利润分配与关联度规则"，在OECD的构想中，支柱一意在从宏观角度出发，设计一套符合数字经济时代的税收规则。支柱一将市场和数据作为一种可以促进产品增值的要素来看待，关注的对象主要是跨国企业，尤其是跨国的互联网巨头。由于数字经济下的企业经营模式已经发生较大变化，传统的"物理存在"完全可以被各个地区的互联网终端取代，对于通过网络提供服务和产品的互联网企业而言，生产和销售产品不再需要在某个国家设立常设机构，数据本身就是其创造利润的载体。而在市场国税收管辖权暂时不明晰的情形下，跨国企业还进一步有选择地在低税国和地区设立子公司，借此将利润留存在所谓"避税天堂"，从而实现集团利益的最大化。在此背景下，如何确保大型跨国企业除了在居民国足额缴纳税收外，兼顾市场国对这些企业在经营地获得超额利润的征税权，便成为支柱一关注的核心问题。

支柱二的关注重心在于协调各国税率，设置一个普适的全球最低税率。这一方案的出发点是一些国家为了吸引外国投资、促进本国某些产业的发展，往往选择采取调低税率的方式，但这种情形会导致相同产业类型的国家在减税问题上进行恶性竞争，相互比拼谁的税率更低。上述情景最终导致跨国企业获得了最大利好，市场国政府失去了这部分税收，而其他保持正常税率的国家也降低了税收收入。在"逐底竞争"（Race-to-the-bottom）的影响下，高税国普遍希望对低税国采取一定形式的限制，而高税率的国家又大多为美国、法国等发达国家，因此 OECD 支柱二重点提出了设置全球最低税率的倡议。

2. 方案的政策应对

支柱一承认市场国作为数据提供国对于征税权重新分配的诉求，关于税权划分也有许多不同的提案和理论。英国在2017年就提出了"用户参与理论"，强调以用户对企业的价值贡献来分配利润；美国则提出了"营销型无形资产"概念，将客户数据归为无形资产，意在建立利润和数据等价值要素内在的功能性联系；印度等20余个发展中国家还提出了以"显著数字存在"为核心的提案，为利润分配设定了一系列相应指标。

欧盟和印度对支柱一有着浓厚的兴趣，但由于欧盟内部尚未就如何基于支柱一的原则设置数字服务税达成一致，部分欧盟成员国转而通过国内立法的方式率先推出本国的数字服务税。[①] 尽管这些国家的数字服务税实践还有许多待完善之处，但这些"急先锋"显然引起了更大范围的对数字服务税的讨论与关注，加上2020年新冠肺炎疫情对许多国家的财政状况造成打击，并且使得BEPS包容性框架的成员加快了对数字经济征税的全球方案的设计，

---

① 截至2020年10月，大约一半欧洲的OECD国家已经宣布、提议或实施了数字服务税，其中，奥地利、法国、匈牙利、意大利、土耳其和英国已实施数字服务税，捷克、波兰、斯洛伐克和西班牙已经公布了实行数字服务税的提案，拉脱维亚、挪威和斯洛文尼亚已经正式宣布或表示打算实施这种税收。

一年多以来，更多政府开始关注对支柱一规则的研究。

相较于欧盟对于数字服务税的浓厚兴趣，美国更侧重于对支柱二全球最低税的研究。这一方面是因为，美国作为许多跨国数字巨头企业的居民国，在传统规则下已经享有了居民国征税权，因此不愿看到数字服务税对自身利益的削弱；另一方面，美国自身也饱受跨国企业利用低税国转移利润、进行激进税收筹划的困扰。例如，由于爱尔兰的企业税率仅为美国的一半，苹果、谷歌等跨国数字巨头通过在爱尔兰等国设立子公司，利用"双爱尔兰三明治"避税安排，在很长一段时间内将利润转移到海外，使得美国失去了数十亿美元的海外税收。

作为全球最主要的盈利转移始发国，出于对自身财政利益的维护，美国一直致力于推动全球最低税率。自从2021年拜登政府上台之后，由于希望推行"大财政"计划，借以缓解美国国内愈演愈烈的贫富分化问题，拜登政府也希望通过支柱二为财政筹措资金。2021年6月，在美国的提议下，七国集团（G7）财政部长达成一项协议，决定推动将全球最低税率设定在15%以上，并加强G7在国际税收体系改革中的合作。

除此之外，从2020年开始，二十国集团（G20）也在审议一项有关全球有效最低税率的提案，即《全球反税基侵蚀提案》，旨在对部分国家为了吸引外国直接投资而展开的税收竞争现象划定底线。

（二）对双支柱方案基础原则的讨论

虽然双支柱数字税改方案的支柱一是从适用范围这一角度切入，但是真正影响其未来发展的第一大基础性问题在于如何确定市场国征税的基本理论依据，而经济关联原则正是国际税收管辖权的出发点。由于关联度问题不仅仅是一个技术性问题，也涉及税权正当性等原则性问题，对征税主体、范围乃至标准等税收要素都有重大影响，因此也导致对这一原则的讨论会耗费较长时间。在实践中可以看到的是，OECD虽然排除了以预提税形式对数字服务征税的做法，却保留了把其视作一种"显著数字存在"下征税方法的可能性，而对直接以销售收入为基础的彻底的市场国征税权诉求又不能完全给予支持。一言以蔽之，OECD其实是试图跳过对原则性和正当性问题的争论，转而关注对技术性问题的研究，然而正是由于国际税收是基于各国共识而建立的一套规则体系，想要略过对原则性问题的讨论，很可能会加大参与各方的争议，反而降低对这一问题的讨论效率，如果未能先解决原则共识问题，则很难将双重征税的风险降到最低，也会影响全球的商业投资环境。

支柱二主要是针对个别地区出现的征税不足情形而提出的，如果这一方案得以实施，那么跨国商业巨头的避税措施将受到较大打击，也可以保障全球各国的税收利益。这一方案从居民国和市场国两个角度提出了四大规则。首先是从居民国一方的立场出发，提出了所得纳入规则（Income Inclusion Rule，IIR）和转换规则（Switch-over Rule，SOR），试图对居民国的税收流失做一定的补偿，这两个原则既允许将在境外已纳的税额进行抵免，同时也补上了现行双重征税规则中的漏洞。其次，支柱二从市场国的角度出发，提出了征税不足支付规则（Under-taxed Payment Rule，UTPR）和应予征税规则（Subject-to-tax Rule，STTR）以弥补市场国的税基侵蚀情况。这四大原则看上去实现了法律形式的公平，甚至还对处于相对弱势地位的市场国进行了关照，然而这一静态的法律形式很难反映市场国在动态发展中对于自身经济建设和税收实质公平的要求。试想，发展中国家作为市场国，希望借鉴发达国家曾经的历史经验，基于市场经济的逻辑选择对某些新兴产业提供税收支持，然而在支柱二的语境下，一旦这些原则以法律形式得以确认，那么发展中国家的税收优惠很可能会低于"全球最低税率"，这种在国内合法且合乎历史惯例的发展政策却违反了基于支柱二的国际税收法精神。一旦这种情形发生，发达国家必然会对这些国家的财政自主性进行干涉，而这种情况，实际上就是以静态的形式上的法律公平压制了发展中国家对于发展权的正当诉求，反而背离了实质性公平原则。

（三）关于双支柱方案公平性问题的进一步讨论

作为全球税收体系改革的重要组成部分，数字服务税和全球最低税率主要针对跨国企业转移利润、侵蚀税基的问题，在一定程度上具有进步意义。但是以欧美国家为主导的 OECD 作为发达国家共同体，其所倡导的 BEPS 行动计划实质上还是在争夺数字经济时代跨国巨头已经创造出的利润的分割权，其本质是存量竞争性秩序。因此，BEPS 行动计划双支柱方案的公平性究竟如何发展仍需要更为深入的思考和讨论。

1. 支柱一方案提倡的新征税权突破了传统税收规则

仔细分析数字服务税，可以发现支柱一方案提出了一项新的征税权，这一方案以公式分配法为基础，旨在解决市场国的利润分配和税基分割问题，而这实际上是对传统国际税收规则的独立实体原则、经济关联原则和独立交易原则的背离。

相对于成熟的传统工业经济而言，数字经济目前还处于初始发展阶段，作为一种创新型经济，国际税收领域税基如何分配，很大程度上是基于国际税收管辖权的初始配置。OECD 支柱一方案的进步性在于，首次对处于数字经济产业链下游的市场国赋予了部分征税权，但同时也不得不与美国达成妥协，保留其作为居民国的征税权，如此看来，以新型所得税形式出现的数字服务税对于全球治理框架的完善只是有限的进步。

但与此同时也要看到，欧盟最初提出征收数字服务税时，是将其定位为解决财政收入困难问题的临时性应对措施，欧盟希望在全球形成对数字经济征税规则的正式方案后，便取消数字服务税这一形式。由于一开始就以临时性措施的形式出现，因此数字服务税也存在较多的局限性。一方面，现有的数字服务税主要是对收入征税，而不是像传统的企业所得税或者增值税那样，对净所得或增值额征税，在这种情况下，数字服务税对获利较少甚至亏损的企业而言，显然是有失公平的。另一方面，由于尚未形成大范围的共识，已有的数字服务税实践也主要是个别国家临时出台的单方面的应对措施，缺乏严谨论证和设计，导致数字服务税很可能无法避免重复征税问题。最后，如果最终无法形成对于双支柱方案的共识，那么不协调的税收政策和各自为政的单边税收方案很可能会加剧类似美法两国之间的贸易争端，[①] 从而

---

① 2019年7月25日，法国官方公布数字服务税法案，而此前15天，美国贸易代表办公室启动对法国数字服务税的301调查。12月，美国政府根据调查结果提议征收报复性关税，还威胁要对其他一直在试图征收数字服务税的国家征收关税；法国也强烈表示将携欧盟一起，报复美国的关税措施。

有可能损害市场国利益。①

2. 支柱二方案全球最低税率的规则有待优化

尽管美国一直致力于推行全球最低税率方案，2020年《应对经济数字化税收挑战——支柱一和支柱二蓝图报告》也特别完善了支柱二方案的设计，但支柱二方案背后依然暗含了对既得利益的保护，也没有对发展中国家基于自身国情采取优惠税制的需求给予足够的重视。同时，尽管 G7 各国对全球最低税率在原则上认可，但这次峰会声明对支柱一方案中的数字服务税只字未提，从中可以窥见 G7 在数字服务税方面的明显分歧，因此，距离双支柱方案的最终落地仍有很长的路要走。

从国际角度来看，世界各国远未就全球最低税率的征收细节达成共识。例如，全球最低税率是否需要对公司所得税的税基进行统一的规定？即使有了最低税率，如何确保各国不会在其他税制要素的定义上出现"逐底竞争"的行为（如在税基或征税对象的定义上做文章，实现另一种形式的避税）？虽然 OECD 提出要对"规模最大、利润最

---

① OECD 于 2020 年 10 月 12 日随同《应对经济数字化税收挑战——支柱一和支柱二蓝图报告》一并发布的评估报告指出，基于共识的双支柱多边措施，对经济的损害将很低，从长期看对全球的 GDP 影响或不足 0.1%；而若缺乏基于共识的应对措施，在"最坏的情况下"可能导致全球 GDP 下降超过 1%。

丰厚"的跨国企业征税,但这种宽泛的描述显然无法确定征税对象的范围。此外,针对以前流失的巨额税收,可以按全球最低税率补征所得税吗?如果答案为"是",哪些国家又可以享有对跨国巨头补征所得税的权力呢?这些问题都亟待解决。

从美国国内看,全球最低税率的立法也充满了不确定性。由于共和党人对全球最低税率多持质疑和反对态度,认为全球最低税率对美国企业不利,会影响美国的竞争力。而在美国,只有得到参议院 2/3 多数同意才能通过国际协议,因此拜登政府想要立法通过全球最低税率协议也并非易事。

3. 欧美积极参与双支柱方案的真实意图

"天下纷纷,皆为利来。"简单分析即可发现,欧盟积极推动数字服务税,是因为欧盟自身就是受美国跨国数字巨头避税行为影响最大的经济体;而美国关注全球最低税率也是由于自身税收利益受到了低税国的损害。

欧盟提出"产消者"的概念,并将"用户贡献"作为经济数字化价值创造的核心概念,是符合数字经济时代市场国税收利益受损现状的。但在数字服务税的设计过程中,征税范围逐渐缩窄,排除了部分行业,这就既保证了在一定限度内尽可能降低跨国数字巨头的税负,又让市场国有税可征,同时还保护了设立在欧盟内部低税国的跨国企业的既得利益。如此，既满足了欧盟和美国的既得利益，欧盟作为全球最大的消费市场之一，又能够在未来利用这套规则通过新征税权获得额外的收益。

此外，欧盟积极推动数字服务税规则的制定，符合欧盟在数字经济竞争中相对落后的现状。欧盟选择用更巧妙的方式参与竞争，即通过直接参与规则制定，努力成为全球数字技术的规则制定者，抑制其他国家确立全球科技主导地位的努力。

而美国联合欧盟进行双支柱方案的设计，在一定程度上是出于维护自身超级大国地位的考虑。通过支柱一方案，欧美发达国家（地区）可以实现对数字经济垄断权的分配；而若是支柱二方案中的全球最低税率真的得以实行，那便会造成对发展中国家自主、灵活选择本国税收制度的税收主权的损害，从而压制弱小国家实施有利于促使自身经济增长和促进创新的税收优惠制度的可能性，进一步实现对弱小国家发展权的压制。

综上所述，双支柱方案对国际税收改革进程具备较大的进步意义，围绕双支柱方案进行多边合作的努力，在很大程度上推动了全球治理框架的形成。但其局限性也较为明显。例如，在跨国数字巨头、居民国、依赖低税率吸引外资的低税国等既得利益团体的掣肘下，双支柱方案仅能实现有限公平。而双支柱方案规则的设计使得欧美国家可以维护自身既得利益并实现在新兴市场的共同获益,却忽略和侵害了广大发展中国家的发展权益。

鉴于此,国际社会需要推动OECD公平确立市场国征税权的适用范围,减少不合理的"圈定"和"圈离",尽量实现征税权的全面公平、税制的简化统一。只有这样,才是真正积极地面对数字经济的挑战,才能更加有效地解决国际税收的基本问题,促进落后国家和地区以及创新型行业自主设计税收规则以促进自身发展。

第二节 数字经济国际税收治理变革的中国应对

综合上述研究,科学建构数字经济国际税收改革的中国应对之策,首先需要阐明中国作为社会主义数字经济市场大国,对数字经济国际税收改革在税基安全、公平和发展三个方面的全面关切,强调系统建构、内外联动,实现税收与经济的"双循环"发展格局;其次才能着重勾画数字经济国际税收改革的中国方案,建立一种基于全球市场竞争与政府合作的技术机制和规则体系,打破霸权主义全球化,打造一种有利于多边主义区域一体化和"一带一路"建设发展的新格局。

一　数字经济国际税收治理变革的战略背景

深刻把握百年变局下的数字经济税改背景，我们可以看到世界格局变化有两个重要体现：一是生产力水平意义上的发达国家总体实力与霸主地位的减退和新兴经济体、发展中国家力量的动态上升；二是以资本主义制度及其对应市场经济为框架、以西方价值理念为基石、以单级化为目标的西方道路正在受到以社会主义制度及其对应市场经济为框架、以中国特色社会主义价值体系为基石、以认同现阶段多级化为目标的东方成功道路的挑战,[①]这种与不同政治道路选择相联系的力量对比变化是大变局中最有积极意义的因素，影响极其深远。

如果说 BEPS 行动计划是为了解决经济全球化下跨国企业税基侵蚀与利润转移的问题，则 New-BEPS 是基于世界多极化现实和经济全球化的困境应运而生的。在此背景下，研究国际税收不仅需要深入探索大变局下经济全球化与逆全球化对 BEPS 行动计划的影响，还需要跳出这一框架，重点转向对深受世界多极化影响的 BEPS 行动计划落地实施的研究。在 New-BEPS 中，要主动研究包括中国在内的发展中国家对 BEPS 行动计划的参与、反馈和影响，

[①]　邓力平. 百年未有之大变局下的中国国际税收研究 [J]. 国际税收，2020（02）.

更多地关注发展中国家的诉求。更进一步地说，中国国际税收研究的重点需要围绕中国在"一带一路"税收合作中的贡献，要防止出现将"一带一路"税收合作放在BEPS行动计划下研究的倾向，尤其是要努力提高中国对国际税收多边治理规则制定的参与度。[①] 具体而言，我国应当立足于促进我国数字经济发展的这一目标，从征税权确立、征税对象、税基分割等方面加快国内税制改革，也要配合国际趋势，在拓展常设机构认定标准、推动全球数字经济规则谈判等方面加强国际合作。[②]

二 数字经济国际税收治理变革的政策要点

数字经济主导地位的争夺战，主要涉及中美技术竞争以及效仿欧盟的数据安全和数字税收保护体系的三方竞争，[③] 这是一种主客观结合的趋势。从产业链、价值链以及各国在全球经济格局中的地位来看，欧盟因为数字经济相

---

① 邓力平.百年未有之大变局下的中国国际税收研究[J].国际税收，2020（2）.
② 邓力平.百年未有之大变局下的中国国际税收研究[J].国际税收，2020（2）.
③ 中美欧竞争数字行业标准制定者：抢占先发优势.网易科技报道.2019-07-30.https：//tech.163.com/19/0730/07/ELAL4C7G00097U7T.html.

对落后而成为OECD方案的主要推动者，美国优势明显因而比较抵触数字服务税，中国则处在中间，跟美国在数字经济发展使得居民享受更好的技术进步方面可能有一些立场上的相似性，但是中国在推动实体经济税收平衡方面又有可以学习欧盟改革理念的地方，所以在欧盟极力主张数字经济税收而美国竭力反对的情况下，中国如何对此进行科学合理的定位是一个巨大的难题。

（一）税基安全与全球反避税竞争和合作

中国要积极参与G20和OECD主导的BEPS行动计划，加强信息透明化和征管机制协调以应对税基侵蚀。

中国是数字经济商品和服务的生产大国和消费大国，基于规模效应，无论是从居民国、来源国，还是生产国和市场国角度，均需要防微杜渐、未雨绸缪，搭建完整的国际反避税规则体系；经合组织的《全球反税基侵蚀提案》为我们提供了很好的多边主义全球性反避税框架，我们需要结合自身国情，完善适应数字经济发展的国际反避税规则，确保国家税收利益，保护经济发展成果。

但是我们同时也应当注意到，包括数字经济国际反避税机制在内的BEPS行动计划，本质上是应对全球金融危机引起的财政危机的应激反应，其首要目标在于建立针对跨国公司避税的全球性反避税大联盟，以保障税基安全和财政基础；然而，忽视不同财政体制和不同发展状况的"一刀切"的反避税大潮，极易助长一些国家的保护主义、利己主义的反全球化思潮，容易导致反避税滥用，破坏总体营商环境，有损全球经济的长期稳定健康发展。作为财政收入形式更加多元、财政体制更加健全的中国，财政和经济发展的韧性在新冠肺炎疫情危机下更加凸显，在设计国际反避税政策的时候，尤其是要科学测算"引进来"和"走出去"经济中跨国公司的避税总量，做好反避税的战略评估，审慎规范实施反避税措施，避免形成过度执法和国际反避税恶性竞争，建构更加有利于长期经济稳定发展的环境友好的国际税收政策体系。

（二）税基公平与全球数字和工业经济大循环

中国要推动改革方案扩大公平规则的形式完整性，从工业经济到数字经济全产业链上设计公平的税收管辖权，以在根本上实现数字经济和实体经济的税基平衡。

双支柱方案中的提案和规则大多是由数字经济消费大国提出的，在全球经济增长趋缓的背景下，不排除有些国家为减轻财政压力，从本国政策偏好的角度来提出提案的可能性，因此我们应理性看待双支柱方案。基于中国的社会主义国家性质、经济现状和未来发展，我们有必要确立一种更有利于数字经济生产和消费平衡、数字经济和实体经济协调发展的政策安排。

其中，税基公平政策的起点应当是，明确消费是数字经济的战略贡献者，其本质是基于国家经济形成的生产能力转化而来的使用力和消费力，数字经济的发展是由生产者、使用者/消费者和国家/政府共建的结果，数字经济的收益也应当由这些利益相关者共享，不应该损失其在共建成果中的利益份额，但任何一方也不应当攫取不当的超额收益。基于此，税基公平政策的原则应当是，还原并创新（国际）税收理念，通过传统税收体系的进化来适应数字经济的发展，积极推动将市场国征税权回溯至工业经济，而不是另辟蹊径对数字经济进行"圈离式"改革隔断经济联系；改进后的税制体系应一体化适用，以克服众多方案的多重弊病，有利于工业经济和数字经济公平一体的全球化大循环。从税基公平政策的价值角度判断，长期以来中国受累于工业经济阶段国际税收管辖权配置的不公平，在未来可见阶段中国仍将致力于保持工业经济与数字经济的平衡发展，加上中国的社会主义国家性质和"一带一路"倡议的进步性，将立足国内和国际生产和消费的平衡，从而实现国内循环和国际循环的可持续发展。①

---

① 王卫军，曹明星.数字经济国际税收治理：机制挑战与系统应对.工作论文，未刊稿。

（三）税基发展与落后地区和新兴行业的经济成长

中国要基于共建"一带一路"理念倡导"税基共建与利润共享"，理性对待税收优惠、帮助发展中国家强化完整的财政能力建设，从实质意义上促进落后地区的经济增长和新兴行业的普惠性发展。

如果对目前OECD主导的数字经济国际税收治理变革进行定性，其应该是一种消极的积极。就总体方案的积极性而言，它使市场国与传统的来源国相区别，以获取一种主动的、正当的税收管辖权，从而推动税收利益的再平衡，改变了原来的国际税收治理理念和格局；就总体方案的消极性而言，其在谋求一种形式化的公平，忽略了落后地区和新兴经济市场发展动力的特殊性要求，有可能在实质上阻碍和伤害它们的健康发展。为此，我们要正确评价落后地区和新兴行业的税收优惠政策，科学制定税收收入与经济成长的长期战略。

经合组织支柱二方案的前提与核心在于确定"全球最低税率"，名义上将对所有国家产生正向收益。然而，静态形式的规则往往无法反映动态发展的实质公平需求，如果规则被理想化和滥用，将大大限制发展中国家的发展权，新兴数字经济行业发展也将面临相似的局面，即正当的自主性特别发展需求成为不正当的、没有规则支持和保护的行为。支柱二方案在法律的形式层面保障了居民国和来源国的税基安全和公平,但前提是在经济活动正常发生的情况下,也就是说方案规则适用于经济活跃的地区和行业。如果落后地区和创新行业需要启动经济、促进增长,基于历史经验(其实也是市场经济的资本逻辑),往往亟须国家乃至国际给予初期资本投入所需要的财政税收优惠支持,这就毫无疑问会出现单边、双边乃至多边的有效税率低于 OECD 设定的所谓"全球最低税率"的情形。这些情形又必然招致支柱二方案中反避税规则的不正当干涉,形成对正当发展权的压制。由此,除了完善支柱二方案的排除规则外,当下亟须的是,在"一带一路"建设中积极推动并帮助发展中国家强化国家能力建设、建立更加完整的财政体制,以更丰富的财政资源弥补和支撑公共服务成本,保持更好的财政韧性,才能有效实施财政税收优惠政策,实现产业发展和经济增长的最终目标。

三 数字经济国际税收治理变革的政策机制设计

基于数字经济国际税收治理变革的战略背景的梳理和政策体系的建构,笔者认为有必要提出基于中国现实国情和未来发展的改革路径:一方面克服一些国家采取的单边主义政策造成的市场障碍,另一方面也突破

OECD方案的保守性和局限性，推动构建有利于"一带一路"建设的国际经济竞争与合作新模式。

回到OECD和G20提出的"利润应在经济活动发生地和价值创造地被征税"的基本原则，从促进市场国和居民国、来源国与居民国等相关利益主体共同发展、共建税基、共享税源，打造人类利益命运共同体的目标出发，中国提出了税基共建与利润共享的数字经济国际税收方案，也就是New-BEPS方案。[①]在"一带一路"包容性增长理念推动下，New-BEPS打造的是一种更具主动国际合作特征的增长型和共享性秩序，并将以简单、确定、高效和公平的国际税制推动税基共建与利润共享，有利于经济发展和实质性社会公平秩序的实现。New-BEPS方案的基本思路是将支撑现行国际税收规则判定标准的两大基石（常设机构规则和独立交易原则）深化整合调整为个人存在原则。对应于独立交易原则下现行国家对常设机构进行税务检查来实现，在新机制下则以国家对个人纳税的有效激励原则来实现。这样，以个人与企业层面的税收竞争来实现独立交易原则，在市场竞争中实现个人利益与企业利益、国家利益的统一，实现利润在经济活动发生地和价值创造地被

---

① 曹明星.为国际税收新秩序贡献中国智慧[N].中国财经报，2016-09-13（06）.

征税，实现税基共建与利润共享。

上述方案的具体操作要点如下。跨国数字企业按居民国税法自行计算全球应纳所得税额，跨国企业根据全球用户（包括产消者、经常客户）的贡献自行分配所得税并缴纳到用户所在地国库，用户凭跨国企业分配给自己的所得税向当地税务部门申请抵扣个人所得税或享受更多更优的社会公共服务。在这一过程中，跨国企业是有激励向用户分配所得税的，因为这样可以赢得更多的用户、扩大市场规模，用户因此得到更多实惠，居民国也乐见其成，市场国也得到税收利益，实现四全其美。[①] 这种设计应当分两个阶段来实现。第一阶段以"窄、轻、稳"为基本原则。"窄"指适用面不宜宽，要从大型跨国数字企业来试点推进，而后根据实际情况进行调整逐步拓展。"轻"指给用户等分配的所得税额不宜过大，否则容易造成居民国税收波动，推进难度会比较大；而从运行机制上来讲，只要打开市场国分享税收的竞争市场，市场国的利益就会不断扩大。"稳"指方案的推进要稳，世界经济合作需要稳定的外部大环境，国际税收的传统需要尽可能坚持，国家间的合作也要稳步推进。第二阶段以"中、平、活"为基本原

---

① 王卫军，朱长胜.应对数字经济的挑战：从生产增值税到消费生产税[J].税务研究，2020（12）.

则。"中"要达到税制的中性原则，要让各类企业（不仅是数字企业，还包括传统企业）在市场竞争中决定用户、资本和技术等各类要素的价格，开创各类要素所有者的税收竞争市场。"平"要在市场竞争中实现平等、公平的结果，达到企业、用户、市场国、居民国公平享有发展成果。"活"就是要跳出税基争夺的狭隘目标，保障经济发展的活力，创造经济发展的动力，促进人类命运共同体的兴旺。[1]

---

[1] 曹明星.数字经济国际税收改革的方案博弈与中国抉择.工作文稿.

参考文献

1. Brauner, Y. "Developments on the Digital Economy Front: Progress or Regression?" [J]. *Intertax*47, No. 5 (2019).
2. Bruins, Einaudi, Seligman, Sir Josiah Stamp. "Report on Double Taxation, Submitted to the Financial Committee of League of Nations" [R]. (1923). https://www.jstor.org/stable/2341293.
3. CUI Wei. "The Digital Services Tax as a Tax on Location-Specific Rent" (2019). https://papers.ssrn.com/sol3/papers.cfm?abstract_id=3321393.
4. Haslehner, W.C., Kofler, G.W., Pantazatou, K. *Tax and the Digital Economy: Challenges and Proposals for Reform* [M]. Kluwer Law International, 2019.
5. J. Becker, J. Englisch. "Taxing Where Value Is Created: What's 'User Involvement' Got to Do with It?" [J]. *Intertax* 47 No. 2 (2019).
6. KPMG, TUAC, G24, Johnson & Johnson, P&G, PWC, SCTI, USCIB, et al. "Comments on OECD Public Consultation Document on Secretariat Proposal for a 'Unified Approach' under Pillar One" [R]. Paris. 2019.
7. Michael P. Devereux, François Bares, Sarah Clifford, et al. "The

OECD Global Anti-Base Erosion Proposal" [R]. Oxford University Centre for Business Taxation. 2020.

8. OECD. "Tax Challenges Arising from Digitalization: Report on Pillar One Blueprint" [R]. Paris: OECD, 2020.

9. OECD. "Tax Challenges Arising from Digitalization: Report on Pillar Two Blueprint" [R]. Paris: OECD, 2020.

10. Pistone, P., Weber, D. (eds). *Taxing the Digital Economy：the EU Proposals and Other Insights* [M]. IBFD. 2019.

11. Reuven S. Avi-Yonah, Kimberly A. Clausing. "Toward a 21st Century International Tax Regime" [J]. *Tax Notes International*, August 26, 2019.

12. Sanghvi, R.C., Ajwani, N.A., Sanghvi, R.R. *Digital Taxation：a Holistic View* [M]. Taxmann, 2019.

13. Spencer, D.E. "The OECD Work Program：Tax Challenges of the Digitalization of the Economy" [J]. *Journal of International Taxation* 31 No. 2 (2020).

14. 白彦锋，岳童．数字税征管的国际经验、现实挑战与策略选择 [J/OL]．改革，2021（02）．

15. 曹明星．BEPS 方略：新威权主义重构国际税收秩序的集结号？[J]．国际税收，2014（07）．

16. 曹明星．数字经济国际税收改革的方案博弈与中国抉择．工作论文．

17. 曹明星．New-BEPS：提供"一带一路"理念下的国际税改方案．http：//News.cufe.edu.cn/info/1004/11172.htm.

18. 曹明星．OECD 数字税改方案述评：理论阐释、权益衡平与规则建构 [J]．税务研究，2021（06）．

19. 崔虹．拨开迷雾：数字经济下税收管辖分配规则三重挑战的应对

[J].国际经济法学刊,2020(04).

20. 崔晓静.论中国特色国际税收法治体系之建构[J].中国法学,2020(05).

21. 邓力平.百年未有之大变局下的中国国际税收研究[J].国际税收,2020(02).

22. 邓力平,曹明星.数字经济时代的国际税收治理研究:中国视角[J].工作论文.

23. 高海波.数字帝国主义的政治经济学批判——基于数字资本全球积累结构的视角[J].经济学家,2021(01).

24. 龚辉文.数字服务税的实践进展及其引发的争议与反思[J].税务研究,2021(01).

25. 国务院发展研究中心"国际经济格局变化和中国战略选择"课题组,李伟,隆国强,等.未来15年国际经济格局变化和中国战略选择[J].管理世界,2018(12).

26. 韩霖.数字经济背景下对税收管辖权划分的思考——基于价值创造视角[J].税务研究.2017(12).

27. 科尔曼·茉莉,刘奇超,陈明(译).经济数字化背景下常设机构的规则调整:一个总体框架[J].国际税收,2018(06).

28. 孔令全,黄再胜.马克思劳动价值论之数字经济时代拓展——西方资本主义社会数字劳动价值创造研究[J].广东行政学院学报,2018(02).

29. 蓝江.从物化到数字化:数字资本主义时代的异化理论[J].社会科学,2018(11).

30. 励贺林,姚丽.法国数字服务税与美国"301调查":经济数字化挑战下国家税收利益的博弈[J].财政科学,2019(07).

31. 励贺林. 对数字经济商业模式下收益归属国际税收规则的思考[J]. 税务研究, 2018（07）.

32. 廖体忠. 公平和现代化的国际税收体系：回顾与探索[J]. 国际税收, 2019（11）.

33. 廖益新. 数字经济环境下营业利润课税权的分配[J]. 厦门大学学报（哲学社会科学版）, 2017（04）.

34. 刘芳雄, 陈虎. 全球反避税形势及中国反避税制度的完善之道[J]. 税务研究, 2019, 411（04）.

35. 刘建徽, 周志波. 经济数字化与全球税收治理：背景、困境与对策[J]. 宏观经济研究, 2020（06）.

36. 刘奇超. 论经济数字化国际税收改革中"统一方法"的规则设计[J]. 国际税收, 2020（02）.

37. 罗珉, 李亮宇. 互联网时代的商业模式创新：价值创造视角[J]. 中国工业经济, 2015（01）.

38. 罗秦. 国际税收治理从双边到多边的演进：新格局、新挑战及新趋势[J]. 国际税收, 2021（01）.

39. 马述忠, 郭继文. 数字经济时代的全球经济治理：影响解构、特征刻画与取向选择[J]. 改革, 2020（11）.

40. 玛丽安娜·马祖卡托. 企业家型国家：破除公共与私人部门的神话[M]. 商务印书馆, 2017.

41. 潘楠. 我国与"一带一路"沿线国家合作型国际税收治理[J]. 南京工程学院学报（社会科学版）, 2020（03）.

42. 裴长洪, 倪江飞, 李越. 数字经济的政治经济学分析[J]. 财贸经济, 2018（09）.

43. 乔晓楠, 郗艳萍. 数字经济与资本主义生产方式的重塑——一个政

治经济学的视角 [J]. 当代经济研究，2019（05）.

44. 汝绪华，汪怀君. 数字资本主义的话语逻辑、意识形态及反思纠偏 [J]. 深圳大学学报（人文社会科学版），2021（02）.

45. 王娟娟，史碧林. 面向"一带一路"区域构建"双循环"产业体系——基于六大经济走廊的分析 [J]. 东北亚经济研究，2021，5（03）.

46. 王玉柱. 数字经济重塑全球经济格局——政策竞赛和规模经济驱动下的分化与整合 [J]. 国际展望，2018，10（04）.

47. 谢富胜，吴越，王生升. 平台经济全球化的政治经济学分析 [J]. 中国社会科学，2019（12）.

48. 约阿希姆·恩利施，刘奇超，沈涛，肖畅，任雪丽. 国际有效最低税：对全球反税基侵蚀提案（支柱二）的分析 [J/OL]. 海关与经贸研究，2021（06）：1-23.http：//kns.cnki.net/kcms/detail/31.2093.f.20210628.1319.002.html.

49. 张巍，郭墨. 数字经济公平征税的若干问题探析 [J]. 税务研究，2021（02）.

50. 张泽平. 数字经济背景下的国际税收管辖权划分原则 [J]. 学术月刊，2015（02）.

51. 张智勇. 数字服务税：正当的课税抑或服务贸易的壁垒？[J]. 国际税收，2020（04）.

52. 朱青，杨宁. 关于 OECD 应对经济数字化国际税收改革方案的评论 [J]. 国际税收，2020（08）.

53. 朱炎生. 经合组织数字经济税收规则最新提案国家间利益博弈分析 [J]. 国际税收，2019（03）.

附录

International Tax Governance in the Digital Era: A Chinese Perspective[①]

Prof. Dr. DENG Liping
Distinguished professor of Xiamen University and professor of Xiamen National Accounting Institute; Vice president of China International Taxation Research Association.

Prof. Dr. Bristar Mingxing CAO
Director of China International Tax Center (CITC) at the Central University of Finance and Economics (CUFE); member of the Executive Committee at the IFA.

---

① Sincere thanks to Ms. HAN Lin of *China International Taxation Magazine*, Dr. DU Jianwei of China State Taxation Administration, Mr. WANG Weijun of STA Hainan Bureau, Mr. LIU Qichao of STA Shanghai Bureau, for the consults and contribution in drafting the article.

115

This article aims to depict from a Chinese perspective international tax governance in the digital era. The first part is an in-depth interpretation of the historical background of the "Great Change"; in this part, the basis, impetus, framework and mechanism of the "Great Change" impact on the key actors and their historical roles in restructuring international tax governance are listed and discussed. The second part is a case study of the era of digital economy in terms of order reform in international tax governance; in this part, current challenges, OECD plans, theoretical innovations and China's concerns and possible policy-making are tentatively elaborated.

Introduction

The world is undergoing an "unprecedented big change in a century", and the new kinetic energy represented by the digital economy will render innovative destruction to the traditional international economic pattern; the way how the emerging international economic pattern responds to the historical impact of the new kinetic energy on the development of the world economy, and correspondingly establishes an new order of development, will bring different challenges and opportunities to the formulation of international taxation policies in each economic zone and various countries.

1 Historical Background of the Reform of International Tax Governance: A General Analysis of the "Unprecedented Change in A Century"

In recent years, China President Xi Jinping has put forward the grand concept of "Unprecedented Big Change in A Century " (herein after as the Great Change) on many important occasions, depicting the strategic vision and profound insights on the status quo and development trends of current times. This is the international background in which we are studying various issues in the reform of international tax governance. This article discusses three points in the study of international tax governance under the "Great Change": first, to clarify the importance of the "Great Change" to international tax governance; second, to interpret the overall impact of the "Great Change" on the development and changes in the field of international taxation; third, to re-measure and timely adjust the reforms of international tax governance against the "Great Change"[1].

1.1 Global background of international tax governance under the "Great Change"

The important conclusion of the "Great Change" can

---

[1] See Deng Liping. *Research on China's International Taxation under the Great Changes Unseen in a Century.* China International Taxation, 2020-02-09 pp.3 et seq.

be understood from three dimensions: the connotation of the times, the historical position and the recent characteristics.

1.1.1 The contemporary connotation of the "Great Change"

President Xi Jinping pointed out in the Nineteenth National Congress of the Communist Party of China, "The world is in a period of great development, big changes, and major adjustments. Peace and development are still the themes of the times. The world today is the one of in-depth multipolarity, economic globalization, social informatization, and cultural diversity." This is an important judgment to interpret the current world pattern which can be elaborated in the following three aspects:

First, "Great Change", "Great Development" and "Great Adjustment" appear at the same time. The developments and adjustments at specific stages demonstrate specific trends, and only by knowing the general trend of the world can the global pattern change be discerned in-depth. Throughout today's world, "peace and development" is the primary prerequisite for understanding the general trend of the world; as a basic trend, "Great development" will inevitably bring about "Great Change" and will therefore call for "Great Adjustments." Since the times are advancing, science and technology are developing, and the lagging-behind are catching up, our world shall stand up to the dynamic of the current "Great Development, Great Change, and Great Adjustments"; all these factors are having profound impacts on current international relations, which demands the adjustment and even the reshaping of the international rules which sustains the international tax order.

Second, the "Great Change" is forming a new world pattern, and it is the "Great Change" that reflects its dynamic characteristics. Regarding the world pattern brought about by the "Great Change", the description for many years was originally "economic globalization, world multi-polarization, and technology informatization." After the turn of the century, it was summarized as "economic globalization, world multipolarization, technological progress, and new global issues." The report of the 19th National Congress of the Party was further adjusted to the four characteristics of "world multipolarization, economic globalization, social informatization, and culture diversity". At the Asian Civilization Dialogue Conference in May 2019, President Xi Jinping put "Cultural Diversity" before "Social Informatization". By carefully analyzing these changes in the characteristics of the world pattern, we can dynamically understand the profound connotation of the "Great Change": "Multi-polarization of the world" is at the forefront of the characteristics, indicating that the political relationship between countries is the primary factor affecting the development of the world, it not only highlights the confrontation between the cooperative win-win model and the isolationism, but also emphasizes the coexistence and competition of different political development paths; "Economic globalization" is a second characteristic, it not only demonstrates that globalization is still the mainstream, but also warns that globalization is facing protectionism and unilateralism; the thirdly emphasis on "cultural diversity" highlights the role of the deepest and most important cultural factors in international relations, and out-posts the importance of deepening communication between different cultures under the Great Change; the fourthly concern on the evolution of "social informatization", which is characterized by the emerging technologies represented by big data, cloud computing, and artificial intelligence, discloses the profound changes brought out to the mankind, implicating optional growth momentum and development paths for the development of many countries.

Third, we shall discern the dialectical relation between the "changing" and "unchanging", the "changed" and "unchanged" (factors) in the Great Change. As far as the "changing" and "unchanging" are concerned, what is unchanged is the contemporary theme of "peace and development". It is the mainstream willingness of all countries to seek common ground while reserving differences through win-win cooperation. It is also the basic position of sovereign states to participate in international exchanges based on their own interests. In the Great Change, the "unchanging" factor must be persisted for long. As far as the "changed" and "unchanged" are concerned, the characteristics of the current world pattern are "changed" relatively to the past and "unchanged" relatively to the future. We must be able to anticipate changes and plan ahead for growth and fairness, which is of great significance to the research of international tax governance.

1.1.2 The historical position of the "Great Change"

Since the end of 2017, President Xi Jinping has positioned the big pattern brought about by the big changes as the "Great Change" and added the definition of "unprecedented in a century". What is meant by " big change unprecedented in a century", it must be examined in the long course of history. In short, it means both a hundred years and hundreds of years.

From a perspective of one hundred years, this is the centenary of the Chinese nation from "striving for national independence and liberation of the people" to "realizing the prosperity of the country and prosperity of the people". The Great Change correspond to the changes in the international environment and the new world pattern in the past century in which the Chinese nation has been continuously reviving and rising.

From the dimension of hundreds of years, scientific socialism has changed from fantasy to science, and human society has undergone tremendous changes. This is the centuries of socialism experiencing exploration, development, falling into a low tide and flourishing again. The most distinctive of these are Chinese characteristics practice of socialism. Socialism is constantly improving and vigorous in the contest with capitalism. The progress of socialism with Chinese characteristics has enable socialism bring hope to mankind never more than today. The longitudinal dimension of "Hundreds of Years" highlights the new opportunities that the road of socialism with Chinese characteristics has brought to the world.

1.1.3 The current characteristics of the "Great Change"

To understand the Great Change, we must not only analyze the basic connotation of the specific period and the historical position, but also shall look forward to forecast the characteristics that can foresee the future world. At the BRICS Business Forum on July 25, 2018, President Xi Jinping summarized the international impact of the "Great Change" on the next ten years as "new and old kinetic energy conversion, power contrast and rebalance, and profound system remodeling". "The next ten years will be a key decade for the conversion of the old and new kinetic energy of the world economy"; "The next ten years will be the decade in which the international pattern and the comparative evolution of power has accelerated"; "The next ten years will be a decade of reinvention for a profound global governance system." This is an important basis for understanding the trend of the Great Change in the next decade and its impact on international tax governance. By studying carefully these incisive expositions, combined with the characteristics of the era of Great Change and the understanding at a historical level, we can have a comprehensive understanding of the "Great Change", and have a dynamic sense of history and sense of the times.

1.2 The impact and characteristics of the "Great Change" on international tax governance

Corresponding to the connotation of the times and the recent characteristics of the "Great Change", at least four aspects can be highlighted to understand the impact itself and the influence on international tax governance.

1.2.1 Basis: The profound impact of the changing characteristics of the world pattern on international tax governance

From "economic globalization, world multi-polarization, technology informatization" to "economic globalization, world multi-polarization, progress in science and technology, new global issues", then to "world multi-polarization, economic globalization, cultural diversity and social Informationization", the dynamic changes in the world pattern determines the development of tax relations among countries, and call for the adjustment of international tax governance.

First, it should be noted that the world multi-polarization is put before economic globalization, which implies that it is necessary to look at international tax relations from an internationally political perspective. In the process of world multi-polarization, the role of emerging economies and developing countries in global governance is increasing, and the development path with Chinese characteristics is gaining worldwide attention. These forces should have more words in the formulation of international tax rules.

Second, more attention should be paid to the new characteristics of the process of economic globalization. The current globalization has been severely challenged, and the forces against globalization have been rising. International taxation relations are bound to be affected by new changes in the international economic landscape. We should pay close attention to the new manifestations of international tax coordination in the downward phase of the world economy, and promote multilateral and sub-multilateral international tax cooperation in maintaining economic globalization.

Third, the impact of "cultural diversity" on international tax relations should be explored. Cultural exchanges have become an important aspect that affects tax relations between countries. Tax exchanges between countries must be based on respect for the values and cultures of various countries.

Fourth, it should not be neglected that "social informatization" has brought new challenges to the tax systems and tax relations among countries. It is necessary to strengthen tax cooperation in response to new technologies, new industries, and new business models, and promote international tax rules to adapt to the digital economy. Interpreting the above ideas will help us understand the key points of the new reform of international tax governance, and recognize the important impact of political, economic, cultural, and technological factors on the trend of international tax relations and the reshaping of international tax rules.

1.2.2 Impetus: New requirements from the digital economy for the reform of international tax governance

An important feature of the Great Change is the "new and old kinetic energy conversion" of the world economy, which poses challenges to sovereign and international taxation. For example, the development of the digital economy has changed the trade and investment methods of various countries and reshaped the distribution of international interests. As another example, the mismatch of tax location, economic activity, and value creation makes it difficult to adapt the original international tax rules. The fictitious nature of the digital economy is also eroding the traditional principle of tax jurisdiction allocation. In addition, the development of blockchain and tax-related information collection and processing technologies has also promoted the digital transformation of tax collection and administration. For these new issues brought about by the digital economy, two important trends should be seen:

Firstly, in order to jointly face the challenges of the digital economy, cooperation between countries has begun a new journey. From the 2016 Hangzhou Summit "G20 Digital Economy Development and Cooperation Initiative" to the 2019 Osaka Summit "Osaka Digital Economy Declaration", all the major countries in the world attach importance to the development of the digital economy, especially the reform of digital trade rules. We must follow this trend and work with other countries to explore the construction of tax rules in context of the digital economy.

Secondly, there are still disputes over sovereign national interests in dealing with the tax challenges of the digital economy. We must consider issues in the national interest. At present, the scale of the US digital economy ranks first in all countries, China secures the position of the second largest digital economy, and other developed countries and emerging economies are also making full efforts to catch up. The competition for the leading position of the digital economy is a game for national interest, and the process of formulating tax rules for the digital economy is also a process of redistribution of national interests. It is necessary to understand the relationship between conforming to the global digital economy tax rules and the use of taxation methods to accelerate the development of national/regional digital economy. To speed up the reform of the domestic tax system in terms of taxation subjects, taxation objects, tax source administration, etc., it is also necessary to expand the standards for the identification of permanent establishment, to create new profit allocation rules, to split fairly the profits of the digital economy, to bridge the development gap of the digital economy, to promote the global digital business, and to strengthen international cooperation in such areas as economic negotiations.

1.2.3 Framework: the new trend of "East-West / South-North" division in the international tax arena

Another important feature of the Great Change is the

profound changes in the balance of national power, and the world pattern is shifting to "multipolar world" and "multi-party governance system". There are two important manifestations of changes in power contrast and rebalance. One is the decline in the overall strength and hegemony of the northern developed countries and the dynamic rise in the strength of emerging economies in the south and developing countries. The latter's contribution to world economic growth has reached 80%, and the process of reforming the world order has been started. Second, the Western road that is based on the Western concept, the capitalist system and the corresponding market economy, aiming at singularization, is being balanced by the Eastern road, taking socialist system and the corresponding market economy as the framework, the socialist value system with Chinese characteristics as the cornerstone, the recognition of multilateralism as the goal at the current stage. The progress of the Eastern forces associated with different political road choices is the most positive factor in the "Great Change"; the change of the power contrast and rebalance is obvious, and the impact is extremely far-reaching.

This "dual-dimension" change in power contrast and rebalance calls for the adjustment of the existing international tax order. After the Second World War, the developed capitalist countries represented by the United States became the dominant players in international tax governance, dominating the right to speak in international tax governance in terms of personnel appointments, rulemaking, research topics, voting rights, etc.; only the existing international tax order can be accepted. Obviously, the traditional international tax governance system protects more the interests of developed economies. This process was more prominent during the low tide of the socialist movement. It seems that the only way for developing countries to become prosperous and powerful is the capitalist road, and the way for developing countries to modernize their tax systems seems to be only the road of capitalist tax modernization.

But in today's Great Change, with the relative decline of Western economic power and the end of hegemonism, with the progress of socialism with Chinese characteristics, the status of developing countries has continuously improved on the world political stage. This change in power is conducive to developing countries striving for the right to speak in international tax governance. The practice of tax modernization with Chinese characteristics has also provided new options for tax development in developing countries. The new reality requires that the international tax order to coordinate the tax interests of developed and developing countries, and to promote the coexistence and cooperation on different roads of tax modernization. In short, under the Great Change, international tax governance system will be able to experience the impact of the "dual-dimension" changes in power contrast and rebalance. International tax governance system is expected to gradually move towards a new realistic equilibrium.

In this context, it is necessary to shift the focus of comparative research on international taxation from general and common research to individual and specific research, and to realize a joint comparative reference in current tax system research and future exploration of modern market economy. There are two main points to be highlighted here:

The first is to pay more attention to a comparative study of the tax systems of emerging economies and developing countries. In the changing situation, international tax governance is gradually shifting from "Western dominance" to "North-South cooperation", which is an inevitable requirement for the change of "south rise and north fall" forces under the "Great Change". In line with the comparison of the power of sovereign states and the transformation of the right to speak in international taxation, research in the field of international taxation should also expand from taxation research of developed countries and international taxation cooperation between developed countries to taxation research of developing countries, focusing on their advantages and disadvantages of tax law, tax collection and administrative, and capacity building. In the comparative study of developing countries and developed countries, they will improve the ability and level of developing countries in the participation into international tax governance, and further improve the fairness and rationality of international tax rules.

The second is to do a good job in promoting the Chinese tax system and China tax practice in the comparative tax system research, and to reveal the world by comparison. More attention should be paid to China contribution to international tax governance, to demonstrate the advantages of socialist taxation with Chinese characteristics, and to compare the development path of socialist taxation with Chinese characteristics with the development of Western capitalist taxation. It is necessary to prove the need for multipolarization in the world.

1.2.4 Mechanism: New features of tax competition / cooperation and transnational capital flows

Closely related to the characteristics of "new and old kinetic energy conversion" and "power contrast and rebalance" are the new effects on tax competition cooperation and cross-border capital flows of sovereign countries. The international taxation system always consists of these main aspects: Sovereign countries levy tax on transnational mobile tax bases based on tax jurisdiction, this is called the necessary and justified taxation; multinational capital has a tax avoidance motive, and sovereign countries implement anti-tax avoidance, this is called the tax avoidance and anti-avoidance; sovereign states avoid double taxation caused by separate taxation and international tax arrangements, this is called the double taxation relief; sovereign states strive to adopt tax reductions and tax incentives for the mobile tax base, this is called the tax competition; Sovereign countries coordinate to avoid vicious tax competition, to jointly combat transnational capital evasion, or to avoid double taxation for more effective implementation, this is called the tax cooperation. These international tax activities reflect two types of relationships, one is the tax relationship existing between sovereign states, and the other is the tax relationship between sovereign states as a whole and transnational capital as a whole. There are various intersections between the two types of relationships. It must be noticed that these relations have always existed in the Great Change, but they already have new features.

For many years, when economic globalization played a leading role, it was normal for sovereign countries to focus on the distribution of tax benefits and cooperation to avoid vicious tax competition and double taxation. However, when economic globalization progressed slowly, countries faced the downward pressure on the economy, combined with new developments in science and technology, the phenomenon of transnational capital evading taxation and erosion of the tax base has become a regular phenomenon. The contradiction between sovereign countries and transnational capital has become more and more intense, and it has become common for countries to cooperate against aims of profit shifting and tax base erosion. Although these two practices have different emphases, they have in common that there is a decisive trend of economic globalization, and there is a reality that the economy precedes politics. In this case, the sovereign state can be regarded as a whole.

However, in today's era of Great Change, political factors have become stronger than economic factors, and multipolar reality and the difficulty of globalization are intertwined. This has given new connotations to international tax competition in addition to the pursuit of tax benefits. Tax competition in developed countries is often having more protectionist tendency. Corresponding international taxation cooperation also focuses more on the new issues of political multipolarization and counter-economic globalization. Furthermore, while recognizing the contradictions between developed countries and developing countries, we must also see that the coexisting competition between the capitalist market economy and the socialist market economy also affects tax competition and cooperation. In short, the main body of international tax competition and cooperation today is no longer regarded as a "sovereign state" as a whole, but is divided between developed countries and emerging economies, as well as countries that follow different development paths and adopt different market economic systems. This elaboration is extremely important to understand the new trend of international tax competition and cooperation, because there are new variables in the recognition of the degree of tax benefit acquisition and tax disputes between countries under the Great Change.

1.3 The actors and historical roles in the restructuring of international tax governance

At the present stage of the Great Change, "new and old kinetic energy conversion" and "changes in power contrast and rebalance" will inevitably call for "a profound remodeling of the system". This feature is also reflected in the field of international taxation in recent years, in the process of reshaping international tax governance symbolized by the "Base Erosion and Profit Shifting" (BEPS) project.

1.3.1 The historical game of profoundly reshaping international tax rules

Since G20 is gradually gaining more strength and influence in the international arena than the UN, the developed G7 and the emerging BRICS, now G20 has entrusted the OECD for the designing of the BEPS reform plans for international tax governance.

Overall, the BEPS project is the result of the economic globalization. From the launch of research in 2012 to the official landing in 2015, it has contributed a lot to maintaining the security of tax bases in various countries. But since 2016, as the BEPS Action Plans have entered the phase of further implementation in various countries, the international tax order has stepped into the so-called "post-BEPS era." It was during this period that "the multipolar nature of the world's political landscape" has become the primary factor influencing international relations, and "the conversion of old and new kinetic energy" and "the changes in power contrast and rebalance" have profoundly constrained the forward direction of the post-BEPS era. Therefore, the link between the "post-BEPS era" and the world's multi-polarization and economic globalization is an epitome result of the Great Change. It is necessary for us to always look at the reform of the "post-BEPS era" international tax governance in consideration of both the political and the economic factors: on one hand, we must consistently adhere to the BEPS project's against transnational profits shifting and tax base erosion under current economic globalization; on the other hand, we must also keep pace with the important impact of the world's politically multipolarity, to fine-tune and fix the rules of the project. The new world pattern of "the world's multi-polarization stands at the top, followed by economic globalization" means that the adjustment of international tax rules in the face of Great Change is often preceded by rather politics then economy; Russian transition from a positive engagement into to a passive alienation from the BEPS Project is an example of the world geopolitical influence on the formulation of international tax rules.

China is also making efforts in increasing the institutional supply of multilateral governance of international taxation. China has contributed market, capital and technology to world economic growth, and is deeply involved in and is leading the reconstruction of the new world economic order.

China is constantly strengthening the cornerstones of world multilateralism and persistently striving for the establishment of a new order. China's "Belt and Road" initiative and the US trade protectionism have highlighted the difference in the reconstruction of today's international economic order. China's "Belt and Road" initiative is a grand blueprint for inclusive growth and sustainable development of the global economy, and embodies the historic role of creating a community of shared future for mankind. At present, Western countries are still the suppliers of most of the world's institutions, China has changed the profile from an obedient to a participant and then to a co-formulator with fairness and wisdom. The creation of the system is not a one-day effort, such a process should be embodied with the concepts of "political trust, economic integration, and cultural tolerance" which are entailed in the Belt and Road Initiative.

1.3.2 OECD-BEPS framework and the trend of "post-BEPS era"

The impact of the Great Change on the reform of international tax governance is obvious. If the "BEPS era" is the outcome of responding to the erosion of the tax base and the transfer of profits by multinational companies under economic globalization, the "post-BEPS era" is moving forward in synchronization with the world's multipolar reality and the difficulties of economic globalization. Most of the research on BEPS in existing international taxation field is limited to the OECD framework, which mainly discusses the applicability of BEPS projects and the impact on local taxation system under the conditions of smooth economic globalization, but little attention has been paid to the world's multipolar political factors' restrictions on BEPS projects. We must note that OECD has been commissioned by G20 to do a lot of work on the BEPS project, which should definitely be affirmed and respected. But today's international taxation research should continue to examine the impact of economic globalization and de-globalization on the OECD-BEPS framework under the changing circumstances. It is also necessary to jump out of this framework and focus the study on the implementation of BEPS projects that are deeply affected by world multipolarization. In the "post-BEPS era", it is necessary to actively study the participation, feedback and impact of developing countries, including China, on BEPS projects, and pay more attention to the demands of developing countries. Furthermore, international taxation research should of course focus on China contribution to the "Belt and Road" tax cooperation and prevent the tendency of placing the "Belt and Road" tax cooperation mechanism under the OECD-BEPS framework.

1.3.3 "Belt and Road Initiative" Mechanism and the Significance of China Participation and Contribution in international tax governance

Over the years, China has been deeply involved in

the reform of international tax governance, striving to contribute to the global stage an effective "China Plan"; China's participation in international tax governance has achieved a leap from quantitative contribution to qualitative contribution. Since reform and opening up in the 1980s, especially after the accession into the World Trade Organization, China has gradually participated in international tax governance. In the new century, China has participated more actively in the adjustment of international tax rules, demonstrating the active attitude of developing countries in their active actions. From the submission of more than a thousand position statements and suggestions on the BEPS action plan, to assuming the first deputy chairman of the Special Working Group of the Multilateral Convention on the Implementation of Tax Treaty Related Measures to Prevent Tax Base Erosion and Profit Transfer (BEPS), from Astana's "Belt and Road" tax cooperation initiative to the First "Belt and Road" Tax Collection and Administration Cooperation Forum, China has continuously promoted and led bilateral, sub-multilateral and multilateral international tax cooperation, demonstrating China's ideals and efforts on international tax governance.

The world needs to understand the far-reaching impact of China "Belt and Road" tax cooperation on international tax governance. The "Belt and Road" tax cooperation platform and the BEPS Action Plans have both commonality and individuality. Both take into account the interests of developed and developing countries, and both provide a dialogue platform and channel for international tax governance issues. However, the "Belt and Road" taxation cooperation platform stands at a different position, and more consideration is given to the needs of the countries and regions along the "Belt and Road" and surrounding countries (regions). More consideration is given to the demands of developing countries to better meet the requirements of world's multi-polarization. Therefore, for reshaping international taxation rules, we must stand at the height of the impact of the Great Change on international taxation and look at the far-reaching significance of the experience in the "Belt and Road" taxation cooperation.

In all, the efforts made by China in the field of international taxation are to uphold and improve the current international taxation standards. China has never intended to use its own tax modernization road as a standard output, nor will it seek to establish new operating rules that benefit itself. However, China has the responsibility to discuss the improvement of the rationality, integrity and effectiveness of the existing international tax governance system against the era of "the Great Change" in political multipolarization, economic globalization, cultural diversity and social informationization. Such rules-formulating process entails China's great contributions and oriental wisdom.

2 The Order Construction in the Reform of international tax governance: A Case Study in the Era of Digital Economy

The world today is undergoing a major change that has not been seen in a century. The vigorous development of the digital economy has made globalization and international tax governance more uncertain. As a more advanced economic form after the agricultural economy and the industrial economy, the digital economy business model and value creation mechanism are undergoing revolutionary changes, and have become a powerful force to promote industrial structure adjustment and achieve economic innovation and development. In recent years, the competition between digital technology and the leading position of the development of the digital economy has become increasingly fierce. OECD and G20 have made it a top priority to deal with the tax challenges of the digital economy. At present, the G20 has commissioned the OECD to develop the research and design of the international tax policy of the digital economy which has entered the final stage, and the final reform plan will reach consensus as early as the end of 2020, which will have a profound impact on the underlying logic and practical tools of future international tax governance.

As the world's second largest digital economy and the initiator of the Belt and Road Initiative, China digital economy has reached 35.8 trillion-yuan, accounting for 36.2% of GDP in 2019[①]; Seven of the top 30 global internet companies are in China. During the period of full-fledged deployment of developed countries and emerging economies, the competition for the leading position of the digital economy is the gaming of national interests. The process of formulating tax rules for the digital economy is related to the distribution and balance of national tax sovereignty (tax jurisdiction) and core tax benefits. It is an important part of the global governance system and will surely become the key to the future "One Belt One Road" international tax governance. We urgently need to follow the guiding spirit of the China initiative of promoting a win-win cooperation and to actively participate in the reform of the global governance system. At the same time, we must pay close attention to clarifying the relationship between the OECD plan to respond to the challenges of the digital economy and the needs of the "One Belt and One Road" international tax governance. We should plan ahead to streamline the competition-cooperation framework of international tax governance of the digital economy.

---

① See *http://www.xinhuanet.com/fortune/2020-07/06/c_1126199301.htm;* see also *"White Paper on China's Digital Economy Development (2020)" issued by China Academy of Information and Communications Technology on July 3*, People's Daily, 2020-07-06

2.1 Challenges of the digital economy to international tax governance: conceptualization

2.1.1 The concept of digital economy: name and reality analysis

The change of the English concept from digital economy to digitalized economy involves a perspective of understanding the digital economy from the narrow essence to the broader extension, which will affect our basic judgment on the nature of the digital economy and its international tax policy formulation. So, what exactly is the digital economy? This involves the logic from number to data to digital. The number itself has no value, it is an objective mark; but the data is processed through informatization, so it contains value for exchange and use. Then, is the digital economy an information economy? At least it is not the same, because the digital economy is formed only when the information is digitized and transmitted through the physical space, or more accurately, the digital economy codifies the information and transmits it through the digital platform. Only by breaking a limitation in space, especially the physical limitation of the national boundary, can the economic form undergo profound changes. If the information economy is more represented by technology and intangible assets, emphasizing the aggregation and accumulation of value in terms of time -- for example, the inventions of ancient China can be used at the current time--then the digital economy integrates time and space, in particular the space has been docked to achieve direct value exchange. This is the fundamental element of the cross-border development of the digital economy and an important standard that distinguishes it from the previous economic situation. Looking at the world economic pattern under such a new economic format requires an innovative observation perspective from national to global.

2.1.2 Challenges of international tax governance in the digital economy: conceptual conflicts and connections

The digital economy has changed the global value chain construction and profit generation mechanism of multinational companies with different business models such as value chains, value platforms and value stores. Its prominent cross-jurisdictional high mobility, increased scale and reduced entities, the reliance on intangible assets, data as the core production factor, user participation and the increasing importance of the value contribution of data, and other prominent characteristics have further exacerbated the generation and development of tax base erosion and profit shifting (BEPS) issues; under the basic principle of the main outcome of the BEPS action plan, "profits should be taxed in the place where value is created and economic activity occurs".[1] the two cornerstones that underpin the current

---

[1] *Addressing Base Erosion and Profit Shifting*, OECD Centre for Tax Policy and Administration, 2013.

international tax rules are subject to fundamental challenges: First, the nexus rules determining where to levy taxes, in the absence of physical presence, becomes more difficult to determine tax jurisdictions. Second, the independent transaction principle (Arm's Length Principle) that determines how to collect taxes, is impossible to determine value creation of user participation and data. In the end, people even have serious doubts on the subject of taxation, the object of taxation, the method of taxation, and even the nature of the tax types.

The challenge that the digital economy poses to tax jurisdiction and tax base segmentation concepts and rules requires us to re-understand the basic concepts and achieve essential connectivity. In the traditional concept of international taxation, the basis of value creation and economic activity is the residence country, the opposite of which is the source country; whereas the source country (including the permanent establishment) is a concept restricted by the residence country. The source country concept is not strengthening the taxation rights, and on the contrary, it restricts the taxation rights; to put it clear, the development of the concept of resident state is in reality a restriction of the tax jurisdiction of the source country. The conceptual thinking of the resident country determines the basic designing concepts of the current transfer pricing and tax treaty systems.

Looking at the new profit splitting method of the resident

country and the market country under the digital economy, the concept of the market country is firstly a marginalized concept that is opposite to the concept of the resident country, although it is not necessarily a new taxation right, but it is a reaction to the traditional mechanism. For the first time, the industry-lagging-behind jurisdictions are actively striving for rights of tax jurisdiction. In addition, the dichotomy of the resident and source countries or the resident and market countries is an observation in a transnational context; if we make a replacement of the level of national jurisdiction and regard the world as a country, putting countries at the international level into a globalized country, and then scrutinize the endowment or restriction of the jurisdiction of the source country/region and the market country/region, it is easier to observe whether it is justified or whether the boundary is reasonable under current fiscal principles.

In reality, due to the prejudice in conceptual ideas, the current national practice of international tax governance in the digital economy poses obvious challenges. Countries have serious differences on the international taxation mechanism of the digital economy, and some countries have taken the initiative to take unilateral actions; although this self-interested unilateral measure can resolve the immediate urgency, it is undoubtedly increasing the difficulty of international tax competition and coordination of international tax rules.

2.2 Analysis of the OECD plan for international tax governance of the digital economy: negatively positive

As we all know, the focus of the BEPS action plan is to solve the problem of double non-taxation and to repair the loopholes in the current international tax rules, but not to address the regulatory challenges faced by economic digitization itself. For the purpose of multilateral long-term resolution of key controversial issues, the G20 recently requires OECD to speed up the submission of resolution plans under the BEPS framework; after multiple rounds of coordination, OECD finally proposed a "dual pillars" reform plan to respond to the digital economy (OECD, 2019)[1].

2.2.1 "Unified method" of "Pillar 1": a brand-new system?

Pillar 1 "Unified Approach" proposal has created concepts for new nexus and taxation scope rules, three-stage profit distribution mechanism, elimination of double taxation methods, prevention and resolution of tax disputes, implementation policies and collection and administrative mechanisms, etc. In general, most stakeholders in the world are cautious about the new taxation rights, new sales nexus and formula allocation method designed for market countries

---

[1] OECD. Programe of Work to Develop a Consensus Solution to the Tax Challenges Arising from the digitalization of the Economy [R]. Paris: OECD 2019.

by the "Unified Approach", but some commentators affirm the change from the traditional bottom-up (enterprise-government) tax administrative model to a new top-down (government-enterprise) mechanism (Liu Qichao, 2020)[①].

Although the digital economy has not fundamentally subverted international tax governance, it still has a great impact and breakthrough on many principles of taxation. Such increasing non-physical existence, no visible income, intangible asset transaction has a huge impact on the international economic landscape. In this case, it is undoubtedly very difficult to solve the current problems with the original framework of general consumption tax, personal income tax and corporate income tax, because the original taxation rights are all dependent on people or tangibles. The digital service tax, which is now highly recommended by the European Union, regards the revenue of digital transactions as a nexus of measurement. Although it is not yet possible to reach a consensus in theory, many countries have adopted this idea and started the legislative process. This forces us to think about how to redefine value creation and profit division in this new and unique field of digital economy, and even to think about whether the division of direct and indirect taxes

---

[①] Liu Qichao. On the rule design of a unified method in the economic digitalization of international taxation reform: a summary of views, *International Taxation*, 2020-02-09, p24

is necessary. At present, it is difficult to say whether the digital service tax will become a new tax in the future, and the distribution method is still to be explored, but the digital economy has completely integrated the four economic stages of production, circulation, exchange and consumption. It is necessary to break the tradition of concept recognition and mechanism design in international tax governance.

2.2.2　GloBE/GAMT of "Pillar 2": the original sin of tax competition (tax incentives)[1]?

Pillar 2 The "Global Anti-Tax Base Erosion" proposal proposes to establish a rule of "Global Alternative Minimum Tax, GAMT"[2], aiming to ensure that the final effective tax burden of a company is not lower than a certain standard, which will have great impact on the "tax haven" and help enterprises in scientific and rational layout worldwide, thereby reducing the pressure on

---

[1] Under the OECD framework, the act of countries providing tax incentives and creating tax depressions in some tax jurisdiction for economic development is a form of tax competition; in fact, this is at least semantically incompatible with its purpose, because the purpose of these arrangements is in order to obtain a more favorable employment environment and economic development increment, it is not precisely to pursue tax revenue. In this regard, at least conceptually, tax competition should restore its literal meaning, that is, tax incentives (or tax expenditures in the fiscal sense).

[2] Adriana Sánchez Castro. Administrative Capability Analysis of OECD Proposals from the Perspective of Developing Countries [J]. *Intertax*, 2020(2); Bret Wells. Get With the BEAT[J]. Tax Notes,2018,89.

tax competition in various countries and regions; but in fact, the "Income Inclusion" rule, one of the core systems, complements the "Controlled Foreign Company" rules (CFC rules), and the other core system "Tax-erosion Payment" rules are also only the absorption and improvement of results of relevant BEPS action plans; the Pillar does not propose a solution to the problems in the digital business model, and it is still unable to solve many tax problems in the digital economy.

  The important thing to be discussed here is one of the issues that must be faced in the development of international taxation in the Belt and Road, namely the issue of tax preferences or incentives. We believe that, first of all, although the GLoBE scheme has certain progress in anti-tax avoidance to promote tax base balance, but it also violates and challenges the national tax sovereignty; each country has the right to design its own tax system and formulate international anti-tax avoidance measures. The design effect of the preferential taxation system of these countries can be weakened or even nullified, but the sovereignty of each country to formulate taxation rules cannot be deprived. Second, if a GAMT is imposed on a certain country, there are transfer payments within that country and can be implemented between regions, but no country has the power to formulate this rule internationally, and no country will make transfer payment compensation to the affected countries, which is a serious issue of fiscal rights. Finally, a more serious problem is that, the GloBE (especially the GAMT) scheme may severely restrict the development rights of the underdeveloped countries and regions; for example, China and Pakistan have made a bilateral tax arrangement on the development of a certain area/industry and agreed on an extremely favorable tax treatment, the improper intervention of other countries will actually kick away the ladder of development of Pakistan; it is essentially a violation of the growth rights and development rights of underdeveloped regions and emerging industries; therefore, the so-called "harmful competition" needs to be re-examined and re-conceptualized. The fiscal and political economic principles contained therein need to be better analyzed in the future.

2.2.3 The historical game between EU, US and China: is the OECD plan a peasant uprising?

If the current OECD-led digital economy international tax reform is qualitatively positive, it should have been passively positive; in terms of Pillar 1, it is trying to distinguish the market country from the traditional source country for the active and proper tax jurisdiction, as long as the tax burden does not go beyond that the new digital industry can afford, this will promote a rebalancing of tax interests and changes the original concept and pattern of international tax governance; Pillar 2 is seeking a formal fairness, by ignoring the specific requirements of the development momentum of backward regions and emerging economic markets/industries, which may substantially hinder and harm their healthy development and thus be very possibly negative. Until now, the OECD plan to some extent can be viewed as a peasant uprising in ancient China, and it is more like fighting the tyrants to divide the field and finally fall into the strange circle of the dynasty replacing; but if only the OECD plan is designed and will operate in the way of bourgeois revolutions took place in the past in the Western world, by bringing in a new life pattern that is conducive to the development of new technologies and new business models, the civilization meaning in such institutional reform of international tax governance will be more positive.

The OECD program is working hard to respond to the sharp challenges of the digital economy on tax types and tax bases, but this does not mean that countries fully agree with their programs or endorse the EU's digital service tax. Specifically, the United States is more resistant to digital taxes. The EU is the main promoter of the OECD program; the main reason is that, from the perspective of the industrial chain, value chain and economy in the global economic activity pattern, compared with the United States, the digital economy of the EU is far behind, fighting for tax jurisdiction in market countries is a trend of combined subjective and objective. China is in the middle, and it may have some similarities with the United States in the development of the digital economy so that residents can enjoy better technological progress and welfare. However, China shares and upgrades the EU philosophy of fairness in promoting the tax balance in real economy. Under current circumstances, the EU strongly advocates taxation of the digital economy and the United States vigorously opposes it, China position is still unclear, and how to position it scientifically and rationally is still a huge question.

2.3 Theoretical Innovation of International Tax Governance in Digital Economy: Re-understanding of Tax Basis and Re-construction of Fiscality

In general, the focus of the OECD program is to solve the problem of erosion/mismatch of the international tax base of the digital economy, but it fails to provide more reasonable and comprehensive theoretical support, and further research is needed.

2.3.1 Restoration of the multidimensional framework of cross-border transaction

In the discussion of the new framework for value creation, experts believe that the technological-breakthrough innovation and disruptive changes in the business model included in the digital economy make the economic digitization itself "revolutionary". It raises issues and challenges such as intangible capital investment that subverts economic growth logic, the law of diminishing marginal returns cannot be used to analyze digital information products, and the increase of ability to allocate resources with governmental "visible hands"[1]; scholars have also conducted valuable political economic analysis and prove that in the digital economy, the platform community organization relies on extensive collection and transmission of information to reorganize the labor process, i.e., integrating knowledge labor and traditional labor into the new social production system. The labor reproduction process has spawned a "prosumer" with the help of the powerful information penetration capabilities of the digital platform[2]; the ways of value creation, business model innovation and economic rent acquisition in the digital economy era have also changed a lot. The community has replaced the previous technologies and channels as the heterogeneous resources of rent, that is, beyond the original Ricardo rent, Penrose rent and Schumpeter rent, a new form of rent has emerged--the rent of "Connection Dividend"[3].

When discussing profit splitting, the value creation of micro-subjects in the market is often regarded as the focus of international tax profit/tax base segmentation, and a lot of

---

[1] See Pei Changhong, *Political Economy Analysis of Digital Economy*, Finance and Trade Economy, Issue 9, 2018; DOI: 10.19795/j.cnki.cn11-1166/f.2018.09.001.

[2] See Xie Fusheng, *Political Economy Analysis of the Globalization of Platform Economy*, China Social Sciences, Issue 12, 2019 P62—P81

[3] See Luo Min, *the Innovation of Business Model in Internet Era, from Value Creation Perspective*, China Industrial Economics, Issue 1, 2015 P95—107; DOI :10.19581/j.cnki .ciejournal.2015.01.009

effort is focused on companies and markets, but not on the tax source itself. If we look deeply at the unconventional profits and Connection Dividend in the digital economy, we can divide value creation and profit distribution from three levels: the first is the profit due to enterprise value creation, and various elements can be used to request such element distribution rights ; the second is the nation (and its representative, the government) as the overall public personality to claim the right of cost compensation and the right for surplus sharing; the third is the claiming right of contribution and surplus sharing by the overall consumers/producers in such surplus embodied in the special industry/region, or the location specific advantages (LSA)[①]. In this way, it can be observed that any transaction will take place at the three levels of micro, meso and macro; when the total price finally results in the profit, different entities should have the right to claim. The claiming right of the government lies in the public value generated by its expenditures on public service, such value forms a part of the total value through the connection of micro-subject cross-border market transactions, and this value is finally reflected as the price of tax. In this way, in reality, the government's taxation base is derived from itself or the transactions,

---

[①] See CUI Wei, *the Digital Services Tax as a Tax on Location-Specific Rent* [EB/OL].(2018-10-26). https://papers.ssrn.com/sol3/papers.cfm?abstract_id=3321393.

which is the compensation of the government's contribution. Further, it should also be noted that the government's public expenditure is not only in the public economic field, but also in many social fields; the price for public expenditures is mainly recovered by taxation, but the complete government has relatively diversified functions, and its expenditures cannot be fully compensated by the narrowly defined taxes. This leaves more room for exploration in the future in the fiscal policy and practice of the moral government.

2.3.2 Mechanism innovation of profit allocation and tax base division

As far as the innovation of the distribution mechanism is concerned, experts believe that the traditional profit attribution rules are more applicable to the normal income that is attributed to the business functions of various enterprises; but under the conditions of the digital economy, the special geographical advantage manifests itself as the country as an overall platform is creating value based on the location of users, which provides additional benefits for enterprises – Location Specific Rent; thus, digital service tax in cross-border transactions is actually a tax on a particular geographic rent (CUI Wei, 2018)[1]. The real progress of the latest OECD

---

[1] See CUI Wei, *the Digital Services Tax as a Tax on Location-Specific Rent*[EB/OL].(2018-10-26). https://papers.ssrn.com/sol3/papers.cfm?abstract_id=3321393.

reform is that, beyond the "Arm's Length Principle" that is uphold as the basis of international tax law, it proposes a global minimum income taxation policy and a solution to redistribute taxation rights. Further, in the OECD program, sales of market country have become the new tax nexus, but one element of which is quite disturbing, rendering even the enterprises level of new Automated Digital Service (ADS) and Consumer-facing Business (CFB) [1]unable to provide a complete and reasonable explanation of the "unconventional residual profit" (a special kind of Connection Dividend) problem; yet, if we recognize the state/government's macro-producer functions beyond basic public services, we will treat this special dividend as mainly special results of regional government contributions[2]; this is beneficial to transcend the perspective of micro-enterprises to restore the multi-dimensional framework of cross-border transactions and highlight regional advantages and national roles, making it easier to understand that the comprehensive contribution analysis framework with "comparable governments" plus "comparable enterprises" will

---

[1] See OECD. Programe of Work to Develop a Consensus Solution to the Tax Challenges Arising from the digitalization of the Economy [R]. Paris: OECD 2019.

[2] See Jia Genliang, *A New Program for the Discussion of the Role of the State's Economy in the Era of Great Transformation: Comments on "The Entrepreneurial State: Breaking the Myth of the Public and Private Sectors" by Mazucato* [J]. Journal of Political Economy, 2017(5).

be a more profound new international tax law system, and it is possible to improve the current international tax imbalance pattern (IFA China, 2019)[①].

From the perspective of the enterprise in the micro market, the integrated multinational enterprise that forms synergy is regarded as a separate entity, and the arm's length analysis is performed to deconstruct it. The method is actually a cropping of real life, which is not in line with reality, and it still cannot explain how the "unconventional profits" are generated. Although the United States has proposed a "market intangible" approach to rationalize this part, we believe that it is still a solution to the endogenous mechanism of an enterprise market, and it still cannot explain all "unconventional profits." If we change our thinking, re-understand the legitimacy of taxation and the basis of taxation, acknowledge the contributions of the state and its representative government, and confirm that the government establishes a set of taxation systems "by means of expenditure", then the government's determination of taxes, the verification of taxes, and even the inspection and anti-avoidance of taxes are all logically self-consistent and self-contained. Of course, the market system and the government system can be compromised and

---

① See Bristar Mingxing Cao et al, *Public-Private Exchanges: Completion of the Panorama of Comparable Transactions from the Perspective of Government Contribution,* China International Taxation, 2020(7).

connected; taking the Location Specific Advantage as an example, the interests attribution approach of which, to a large extent, solves the problem of how to realize the taxation of different countries in the "unconventional profit" under the innovated residual profit split method.[1]

2.3.3 Reflection on the role of the state, taxation rationality, fiscality and Re-evaluation of the OECD plan

The fundamental question raised by the above discussion is that: isn't the government's tax revenue drawn from private pockets? Judging from the introduction of the multi-dimensional framework of cross-border transactions, a combined micro-macro transaction can only be realized by an overall lump-sum price retained temporarily at the enterprise/individual. The pocket of the private enterprise/individual should not include the return that the state and government

---

[1] The profit split between the state and the enterprise, and between the states, will first be implemented in accordance with the principle of fair share of the fiscal will of the sovereign states. Therefore, the moderated version of the residual profit split method is adopted. On the premise that the profit split of the multinational company does not violate the Arm's Length Principle for aggressive tax avoidance, the residual profit after the initial split by the multinational enterprises will be split again, but this time the focus is on the realization of the overall interests of national representatives, the governments. See Bristar Mingxing CAO: Conflict and Coordination of Transfer Pricing Tax System in the Background of BEPS — Focusing on the principle and method of profit splitting of Location Specific Advantages, published in China Tax Research, Issue 6, 2019, P61.

should enjoy; but still it is often quite normally and easily misunderstood as the private possession by a company or a private person, and the money will be putting into their private pockets, thus the state taxation becomes a grabbing of the private pockets. In reality, there at the meso level shall still exist some surplus of special regions and industries; however, the representativeness of this residual interest is often far more weak in organization, and it is often attributed to the enterprise at the time of division or collected by the government, this is another story and will not be elaborated here.

International tax governance is also forcing us to think about some issues beyond taxation and international taxation itself, such as, can national sovereignty conceived by humans be fully adapted to market development, enterprise expansion, and overall economic growth? how can we pursue the maximization of the human happiness? These require us to consider from different levels of fictional communities of International-Supranational-Universal, to re-construct and re-form the designing concept and rationality. In this sense, we will perceive and say that the EU is a government of supranational to a certain extent, but in terms of fiscal theory, the EU is an immature economy. The significance of fiscality lies in the evaluation whether an economy has a sustainable, healthy, and complete state functions, which are then realized by a moral government and supported by healthy and complete fiscal resources. A moral government can form a government that is different from the original capital or power-dominated government; it serves public needs and pursuit of happiness of all the people, not just the interest parties or groups.

Based on this, when we look at BEPS and its corresponding action plans, we will conclude that its real main function is to seal the loophole of the tax base. We admit that, this is the first time at the international level that a formal cooperative order has been realized, and it is a huge historical progress for the healthy tax base that are vital to the existence of the political powers of various governments. However, because the plans pays no or very little attention on the technology improvement and economic growth for more potential social welfare, it is necessary to add a modifier in front of such Positivity, that is, a negative Positivity, which means that the OECD-BEPS framework is more a system of competition between countries for stock value.

2.4 China's Concerns and Policy Making of International Tax Governance in the Digital Economy: Conflict Coordination between Tax Rights and Development Rights

2.4.1 China's concerns about international taxation of the digital economy

In the context of a digital economy in the Great Change, China's socialist market economy mechanism faces multiple challenges: the first is to achieve balance in the value creation in digital production and consumption; the second is to straighten out the relationship between digital production and physical production; the third is to not only stand up to the competitive challenges of BEPS, but also plan the growth and development under the "Belt and Road" initiative.

In terms of the research in response to the BEPS, Chinese experts have made in-depth discussions on issues such as the reform of the international tax law, the improvement of the income tax system, the reform of the tax collection system and international tax cooperation, and the convergence of international tax rules with domestic tax laws, etc. In terms of the overall policy formulation, experts propose to have awareness of strategic thinking, differentiated subject analysis and forward-looking policy design, so as to not only continue the examination of the impact of the Great Change on the OECD-BEPS framework, but also to jump out of such framework and actively study Chinese issues, in particular, focusing more on the construction of the tax cooperation and sharing mechanism in the "Belt and Road" initiative, in an effort to prevent the tendency that the "Belt and Road" tax cooperation mechanism falls under the rationale of the OECD-BEPS framework[1].

---

[1] See Deng Liping. *Research on China's International Taxation under the Great Changes Unseen in a Century*. China International Taxation, 2020-02-09 pp.3 et seq.

When discussing about China's standing-points, we must on the one hand comply with most of the BEPS anti-avoidance mechanism. But the framework cannot be simply and completely copied to be implemented in China in violating the original fiscal sovereignty and economic sovereignty in some circumstances. Because China has more complicated concerns: for example, how to couple the digital economy with production and consumption? how to realize the integration of value creation and profit division, so as not to cause unfairness? and how to connect the digital economy and the real economy, whether to ring-fence the digital economy from the real economy to reduce the impact of the international tax reform?

On the other hand, we need to make it clear, whether the taxation is to pursue the increase of tax revenue itself, or it is in the greater process of realizing the economic growth – sometimes temporarily sacrificing some tax to seek more economic growth and employment? These are very important and contradictory issues puzzling China. This shall be reflected on the difference between the BEPS strategy and the Belt and Road Initiative. If BEPS is stock-based, competitive, and market-oriented, then the Belt and Road Initiative is more incremental, cooperative, and government-oriented. We need to re-understand the sources of taxation and its justification basis, the role of the state/government and its contribution, as well as what kind of public finance is a healthy fiscality, what kind of government is more moral, and all other profound theoretical and practical problems.

2.4.2 Out of the development trap of "narrow taxation" and "tax de-embedding"

Through combing the theory and practice at home and abroad, we can find that the focus and difficulties of the current international taxation governance of the digital economy are mainly focused on how to reach an international consensus to solve the problem of tax base erosion/mismatch.

OECD focuses its efforts mainly on the field of corporate income tax and seeks to make a breakthrough in it. What we see more is that the reform centers on the stock competition and coordination of the tax itself, and many program designs will inevitably focus on the competition of interest and the consideration of taxation technology; but the reform lacks profound attention to the global economic growth, the design for world economic growth and social sharing is even less common. All these have led to the proliferation of unilateralism, the developed countries are taking the lead, and the tax development has also demonstrated a tendency of "tax de-embedding from economy" similar to Polanyi's "economic de-embedding from society".

Thus, for an economy to have a complete fiscality, it must get out of the two traps of the narrow taxation and the tax de-embedding[1]:

The first is the "narrow taxation". The reason for narrow taxation is that, countries always look at taxation from only one starting point, i.e., from the perspective of micro-enterprises; they do not consider the governments who are contributing in represent of the countries. A country and its representative government shall be a capitalized personality, which is different from an individual person, nor is it a personality that can be simply elected by taxpayers through voting. Compared with the narrow concept of "No representative, no taxation" originated in the formation of modern Western countries, the more complete state form should also include the overall constructive mechanism of "no subjectivity, no fiscality" in the view of updated fiscal principles. In fact, the Western parliamentary system will inevitably lead to narrow taxation, by narrowing the tax revenue and failing to achieve a healthy fiscal subject; a healthy fiscal subject also needs to include broad taxation, such as state-owned assets, profits of state-owned enterprise, national debt, etc. Diversified supplementary factors of fiscality are conducive to enable a country's government function more completely and comprehensively.

---

[1] See Bristar Mingxing CAO, working Report on 2020 Finance and Taxation Salon on New Economy, New Technology, and New Business: Financial and Taxation Policy Innovation in International Taxation of the Digital Economy, Part 4

It is the fundamental basis for providing more and better care for economic and social life, and it also makes the country's taxation more flexible.

Another concept is the "tax de-embedding", which is a problem challenging contemporary international taxation. In current tax-based competition under the global anti-avoidance structure, the starting point and focus of the policy of each country is the stock competition, and it is easy to isolate the tax instead of placing it in the holistic framework of economic development. Similar to the "economic de-embedding from the society" – in which the economy no longer aims at the overall development of society, in the case of "tax de-embedding (from the economy)", taxation now also no longer aims at the overall economic development, no longer considers the economic balance and sustainability, but only pursues the need for the tax base to secure the survival of the government itself. "Tax de-embedding (from the economy)" presents a great challenge to the current international tax law and international tax rules. In this way, we can conclude that the traditional law is a normative and punitive one based on micro-competition, which does not encourage the morally elite public groups; such people exist traditionally in the development of China, they are called the "Shi Ren", whom the Chinese moral governments are mainly consists of. "Shi Ren" aim to serve the overall well-being of the ethnic group or the national people, and they do not pursue the maximization of market-oriented self-interest. The existence of "Shi Ren" is a manifestation of a community's civilization and provides many merits for economic and taxation policies. This factor is of great guiding significance for China's economic development, it will ease the concerns of enterprises and markets in the Belt and Road Initiative, and will help achieve the goals of interactive development of the technology, economic development, and tax sharing among people and regions.

2.4.3 Possible Chinese solutions for international tax governance of the digital economy

Returning to the basic principle of "profits should be taxed in the place where economic activity occurs and value is created" put forward by the OECD and G20, in order to promote the common development and co-construction of relevant taxes by market countries and resident countries, source countries and resident countries, by basing on the goal of sharing tax sources and creating a community of shared interests and destiny for humankind, we propose a Chinese international taxation scheme, Base Exploration and Profit Sharing, which is the New-BEPS scheme[1].

---

[1] See Chapter 2 Neo-BEPS: China's proposal for international tax reform from the perspective of the Belt and Road Initiative, by Bristar Mingxing CAO, *Removing Tax Barriers to China's Belt and Road Initiative*, Wolters Kluwer, 2018

New-BEPS is the embodiment of the "Belt and Road Initiative" principle of mutual consultation, co-construction and sharing in the field of international taxation. Inspired by the "Belt and Road Initiative" concept of inclusive growth, New-BEPS creates a more proactive "going out", growth-oriented and shared order, and will adopt a simple, definite, efficient and fair international tax system to promote the co-creation of tax bases, profit sharing, economic development, and the realization of substantial social justice and order.

The basic idea of the New-BEPS is to integrate and adjust the two cornerstones that support the current international tax rules (the PE nexus and the Arm's Length Principle) into the Principle of Personal Existence. In response to the principle of independent transactions, currently states tax more on residents and permanent establishments, but under the new mechanism, states operate taxation through effective incentives to individuals by cross-type tax credits, i.e., credits will be allowed between consumption tax, individual/enterprise income tax and etc. In such mechanism, the principle of independent transactions is achieved through market competition and government cooperation. This is the aim and result of the Base-Exploration and Profit-Sharing mechanism.

The main points of the detailed operation of the

mechanism are as follows[1]: the multinational digital enterprise calculates the global income tax payable according to the national tax law of the resident; the multinational enterprise distributes income tax and pays to the national treasury of the user's location according to the contributions of global users (including producers and consumers, regular customers); the income tax allocated to local users by the multinational digital enterprise will be brought up to the local tax department for credit of personal income tax or provision of more and better social public services. In this process, multinational companies have incentives to distribute income tax to users, because this can help them win more users and expand the size of the markets when users get more benefits; the country of residence is happy to surrender some tax for resident business enlargement, and the country of users also gets tax benefits which will not be available without such scheme. All four parties get what they desire.

This design should be implemented in two stages. The first stage aims at a "narrow, light and stable" taxation. The "narrow" means that the scope of application should not be too wide; it should be targeted on very large multinational digital enterprises, and then adjusted and gradually expanded

---

[1] See WANG Weijun, *Towards the international tax governance system of market competition, global union (MUP): A Systematic Response to the Challenges of the Digital Economy*, working paper 2020

according to the actual situation. The "lightness" lies in the fact that the amount of income tax allocated to users should not be too large, otherwise, it is likely to cause tax fluctuations in the resident country, and the reform will be more difficult to promote; and as the mechanism proceeds, as long as the competitive market of the user country is invited to share tax, the interests of the user country will become true and will continue to expand. The "stability" lies in the applicability of the plan; the world economic cooperation needs a stable environment, and the tradition of international taxation needs to be adhered to as much as possible, and cooperation between countries should also be steadily promoted.

The second stage shall be based on the principle of "neutrality, fairness and flexibility". To achieve the principle of neutrality, the tax mechanism should allow various enterprises (not only digital enterprises, but also traditional enterprises) to determine the prices of various production elements such as users and capital in compliance with market competition. "Fairness" means that the mechanism should arrive at fair results in market competition, and achieve fair results all for enterprises, users, market countries, and resident countries. "Flexibility" implicates countries shall jump out of the trap of the competition for narrow target of tax base, and shall instead plan for better realization of the economic vitality, for innovative creation of the driving force of economic development, and for sincere promotion of the prosperity of all human community.

Conclusion

In short, under the digital economy, international taxation has both problems of prominent tax base erosion/mismatch issues and also problems of implied significant "tax de-embedding" issues.

The digital economy is the real beginning of global socialized production. Whether it is the integrated "prosumers" or the "connecting dividend" of digital platforms, both value creation and profit allocation are complex and multi-dimensional. All prompt us to conduct a substantial break through from the original micro-enterprise analysis framework, and instead introduce and highlight a more comprehensive and explanatory overall perspective based on regional and national factors.

OECD-BEPS reform framework has a significant historical progress but also has obvious limitations. The digital economy has greatly impacted the basic framework of traditional international tax governance. Focusing on the consideration of solving the problem of "tax base erosion/mismatch", the OECD under the leadership of the EU has turned away from the traditional Arm's Length Principle; the new type of international tax jurisdiction based on the contribution of market countries is substantially progressing and beneficial to balance the national tax interests including developing countries such as China; but because it inevitably has the inclination of offsetting the advantage of the United States in the digital technology and the industrial market for better civil welfare, this framework also implies some conservatism. This complex relationship indicates that the global governance of international taxation has entered a profound multi-polar gaming stage.

China should carefully and actively formulate its own international taxation policies for the digital economy. China should be prudent because, in the reform framework against the "tax base erosion/mismatch", OECD-BEPS has triggered a global game of tax and economic competition, China must protect its own economic and tax interests. China should also be active, because in order to curb the tendency of "tax de-embedding" and to promote technological progress and economic development, the rules must be based on the "Belt and Road" concept for growth and sharing; the new mechanism of "Base Exploration and Profit Sharing" for international tax cooperation innovation and mechanism upgrading should be proposed, so as to leverage government contributions and coordinate tax and economic relations, in the final aim to promote and lead the recovery and growth of the global economy.

图书在版编目（CIP）数据

数字经济国际税收治理变革.理论、战略与政策篇/曹明星著.--北京：社会科学文献出版社，2022.7（2023.2重印）
ISBN 978-7-5201-9107-4

Ⅰ.①数… Ⅱ.①曹… Ⅲ.①信息经济－国际税收－税收管理－研究 Ⅳ.①F810.423

中国版本图书馆CIP数据核字（2021）第194961号

数字经济国际税收治理变革：理论、战略与政策篇

著　　者 / 曹明星

出 版 人 / 王利民
责任编辑 / 陈凤玲
责任印制 / 王京美

出　　版 / 社会科学文献出版社·经济与管理分社（010）59367226
　　　　　　地址：北京市北三环中路甲29号院华龙大厦　邮编：100029
　　　　　　网址：www.ssap.com.cn
发　　行 / 社会科学文献出版社（010）59367028
印　　装 / 唐山玺诚印务有限公司

规　　格 / 开　本：889mm×1194mm　1/32
　　　　　　印　张：5.875　字　数：106千字
版　　次 / 2022年7月第1版　2023年2月第2次印刷
书　　号 / ISBN 978-7-5201-9107-4
定　　价 / 198.00元（全三卷）

读者服务电话：4008918866

版权所有 翻印必究